Acclaim for Al

"This collection of essays is to b[...]
need to feel more normal, seen [...]
come to life with amazing desc[...]
times, these are very relatable stories. We all have our different
versions of pushing limits and seeing what is possible. By sharing
her wild rides, Ammi helps us see the light and the necessity in
seeking more."

—Krissy Moehl, champion trail runner, coach, race director,
and author of *Running Your First Ultra*

"For years I have relished Ms. Midstokke's columns in *The
Spokesman-Review*, both for their wry self-deprecation and for the
fine ear she tunes to backwoods grammar, whether in her homeland
of Sandpoint or on an excursion to Scotland."

—Paul Lindholdt, Washington State Book Award-winning
author of *In Earshot of Water* and *Interrogating Travel*

"Nominally, these stories are about outdoor (mis)adventures, but
I promise you'll laugh, cry, and nod your head in recognition of
deeper wisdom, often all within the space of 600 words."

—Eli Francovich, outdoors editor for *The Spokesman-Review*
and author of *The Return of Wolves*

"Ammi's stories are like her life—unbridled and unique, with
enough humor to hold her (and you) through the sweat and the
tears of living as true to her calling as she can and still remain on
this planet. Do not miss this chance to travel with Ammi, but be
forewarned, it may be contagious."

—Dulcie Witman, LADC, MFA, and owner of Wide Open
Writing

"Regardless of the situation, her brilliantly crafted and precise prose provokes a range of strong emotions. Read one Ammi Midstokke story, and you're hooked."

–Marianne Love, author, blogger, freelance journalist

"*All the Things* is a collage of memoiric musings, a collection of seventy-seven short essays, each crafted with whim, wit, and wisdom. Midstokke, an obsessive long-distance runner as well as a strong and confident forty-something mother, slows down to the speed of solitude in midlife, to contemplate fleeting moments of awareness that arise from a myriad of daily dramas and personal traumas, moments often overlooked, moments ripe for reflection, moments which may illuminate a path to spiritual redemption. 'I am looking for my story, even as I write it,' writes Ammi Midstokke. And aren't we all?"

–Carl D. Barrentine, Emeritus Associate Professor of Humanities and Integrated Studies, University of North Dakota

"While most of us sit back in awe at the things Ammi chooses to tackle and wonder if she's superhuman, this closer look behind the curtain reminds us that she puts her bike shorts on the same way we do (though probably with more clever humor, observation and swearing). That reminder comes in the form of a great read, one in which you'll laugh, you'll cry and most of all, you'll relate."

–Kenny Markwardt, coach

ALL THE THINGS

All the Things

Mountain Misadventure, Relationshipping,
and Other Hazards of an Off-Grid Life

Ammi Midstokke

All The Things:
Mountain Misadventure, Relationshipping,
and Other Hazards of an Off-Grid Life

Copyright © 2023 Ammi Midstokke

Essays were originally published in *The Spokesman-Review* and *Out There Outdoors*

Book design by Russel Davis
Cover design by Kevin Breen
Cover photo by Leo Schmeltzer

ISBN: 978-1-957607-13-9
Cataloging-in-Publication Data is available upon request

Manufactured in the United States of America

Published by Latah Books
www.latahbooks.com

Introduction

AMMI MIDSTOKKE has a flourishing love-hate relationship with misery. She opens doors to it; embraces, loathes and embellishes it; makes fun of it, and learns a thing or two through each grin and grimace. This is what first intrigued me about her and her writing.

"There is a little tiny sliver of fate somewhere between catastrophic life-ending events and nothing happening at all," she suggests. While poring through these pages, you'll realize that she leans largely on one side of that equation.

In September 2014, as the Outdoors editor for *The Spokesman-Review* in Spokane, I reported on a freak mountaineering accident high in Idaho's Selkirk Mountains. Ultimately, a gritty 36-year-old woman was saved by the heroic efforts of her rock climbing partner, a Priest Lake Search and Rescue team and an Air Force helicopter crew.

That might have been the end of the story if my interest hadn't been snagged by the victim's type-A personality.

This gal had a unique perspective on just about everything plus a gift for storytelling and a sense of humor that couldn't be squashed by a 1.5-ton granite boulder. I asked her (admittedly, I was prepared to beg) to grace my newspaper Outdoors section with a column. She jumped aboard and quickly developed an audience eager to read the next installment of her adventures with life, the wilds and living off-grid.

Spokane writer Darin Z. Krogh summed up her allure with this letter to the editor published in August 2017:

"I do not often read the Outdoors section of *The Spokesman*, because I am not an outdoorsy guy. I am even nervous in city parks. But recently I happened to read Ammi Midstokke's column. She seems to be a varied and strange person in a good way. She shoots gophers with a .22, climbs Chimney Rock, rides a bike with a 50-pound load and sprinkles her writing with a you-can-do-it philosophy, tempered by real life disillusions and failures.

"What a strange person she seems to be. I will now regularly read the Outdoors section . . . in order to appreciate (her) curious outlook."

Even if most of her readers weren't aware that Ammi is pronounced with a *long a,* and Midstokke has a *short o*, her words resonated intimately in stories that examine the human condition while tickling funny bones and tugging heart strings.

Her hippie parents and their nonconventional lifestyle get at least partial credit for her instinct to adopt really bad ideas. Why shouldn't a single mom raise a pre-teen daughter in a straw-bale, wood-heated, solar-powered cabin perched on a granite peak with a driveway that passes through heaven or hell, depending on snow conditions and whether the vehicle has enough clearance and a winch?

Why not avoid Disneyland and take that daughter on a summer break trip to Burning Man?

"That's exactly why we need to try it," she explains to her daughter after a sketchy call in yet another outdoor adventure, "to find out how much of a good/bad idea it is."

Ammi is open to just about anything, with a few notable exceptions. For example: "Drinking tea is like sipping on a dead flower that lost its soul. Or supping from a puddle of grass clippings

. . . I realize an entire population of tea drinkers may be appalled by this statement and I commend their Buddhistic ability to be so pleased with so little."

But given the mandatory stiff jolt of strong coffee to wake the Viking blood streaming through her veins, she's game for learning new things every day, and she's willing to bring us along for the ride.

Ammi evolves through the years as she chronicles her devotion to living life to the fullest. Initially she seems obsessed with pursuits that often result in third-degree chafing, or ER visits. "It's never a good sign," she says, "when the radiology staff is on a first-name basis with you and asks how the kids are."

But soon we realize we're tracking her many steps to finding truth and other deep matters, such as love beyond infatuation with a man's mastery of power tools.

She offers thoughtful perspectives on being a mother, wife, sister and daughter as well as on overachieving, aging and mortality. We learn about heartbreak and the healing quality of a dog. She touches on the sobering realities of death, suicide, even extinction. All of this gets sorted out amid her karmic magnetism for chaos.

Learning to coexist with nature outside—and inside—the cabin is a struggle if not a hoot. We get to eavesdrop on her relationships with mice, stink bugs and wasps, as well as the gophers that routinely render her garden to rubble. She tearfully calls planting seeds an exercise in "misplaced hope." But this is only one of many reasons she endorses waterproof mascara.

Ammi demonstrates that emotional growth in finding home, meaning, satisfaction and contentment is possible without losing her badass undertones. In a crisis, she says, balance and fulfillment can always be found in chopping wood.

Although she lives off-grid, she has keen insight to what connects us all. Don't be surprised if you laugh and cry as she navigates her way to life-changing epiphanies. In one of my favorite chapters she details how she is falling in love with her growing child all over again for different reasons than her status as mother. Bingo.

Readers of this book gain great insight into Ammi and life in general. Only her therapist knows more.

—Rich Landers
Spokane, Washington

For

Beverly
&
Beverly

Two lights, One
to show me the way in,
The other,
to show me the way out.

Reflections from Under a Mother &#%!@?! Rock

I TRY TO HAVE A PRETTY BUDDHIST APPROACH to my life, you know, except the part about not eating animals. By and large, I try not to have too much attachment. That being said, there are some things I really just don't want to give up. Like my right foot.

So, as you can imagine, I was not particularly thrilled about the growing reality of this possibility as I lay curled up beneath a hunk of granite the size of a tacky Hollywood coffee table.

There is a little tiny sliver of fate somewhere between catastrophic life-ending events and nothing happening at all. It's about as big as the space my foot was in. And this is exactly what I was considering while I watched daylight fade – somehow I was both damned and lucky at the same time. I wasn't sure if the glass was half full or half empty, but I wished that regardless of the perspective, it was half full or half empty of bourbon.

Back up to some time earlier when two experienced wilderness adventurers of sorts were delayed by a shift in events (and large rocks) that lasted probably less than 4 seconds. I reached to step toward a boulder, and unaware that it was the rarely seen Selkirk Pouncing Boulder, prematurely committed my weight. It toppled forward in that hokey, wobbly way that Pouncing Boulders move down mountains. Unfortunately, I was on it.

There are a lot of places you don't want to be when boulders move. Directly on them or directly under them are probably the worst positions; how I managed to be both of those in the same incident is beyond my comprehension. It does, however, explain how I managed to break both my nose and my foot in the same wacky, stumble-crash-thump-smoosh-thud movement.

"Damn," I thought. "One of those Pouncing Boulders got me."

What I said, I believe, was a string of swear words at a pitch too high for human ears. They don't talk about this a lot in wilderness medicine training, but I'm pretty sure there needs to be some time dedicated to proper accident vocabulary. When the time comes, you need more than a good first aid kit. You need an arsenal of appropriately venomous words to spit at whatever act of God has just attempted to permanently sever you from your appendages. If you run out of words, you are at risk of gnawing off your limbs for lack of anything else to do.

It would just so happen that I was climbing with Jason Luthy of Longleaf Wilderness Medicine. If you're going to have an accident, that's probably the right person to be out with. Unless you know someone who has an Oxycontin stash they're willing to share. Jason didn't have any narcotics on him, so he spent most of the next eight hours keeping the fire going and taking notes on how to improve upon his wilderness medicine seminars. Adding ear plugs to first aid kits was probably a start.

The psychology of being entrapped was something entirely new to me, and I spent much of the evening exploring that while trying to figure out how to keep the emergency blanket over my ample behind. I think they need to start making those in a ladies cut.

First, I wanted to be out from under the rock. Because, as one would guess, it is very painful to lie prone on a bunch of littler rocks while another giant rock crushes your foot.

Second, I was not pleased to be so vulnerable. Either to grizzly bears or Jason's opportunity to get photo evidence of me crying.

(According to official records I've only cried once, in 1984, when I stained my favorite blue party dress with chocolate ice cream and was certain I'd never be able to attend a party again.)

Eventually, I recognized that I was not in a position to change either of those realities, so I ignored them by mourning my party dress and strategizing my pee plan. Because at some point, I was going to have to pee.

Mostly, I found myself needing to ask questions I knew the answer to. I knew rescue was on the way. I knew they would have the best tools possible to free me. I knew they would know what they were doing. In reality, though, I was scared as hell about the things we didn't have answers to. Like whether or not I'd ever be able to wear two shoes again.

For a while, I contemplated opening an eBay store for single shoes. Somewhere out there is a right-footer in a size 38 with a penchant for Italian leather. I envisioned myself as a good Samaritan, donating Jimmy Choo moccasins to leprosy victims.

My fantasy was interrupted by the arrival of the rescue team. They were as good at setting ropes as I was at lying under rocks, and my foot was soon freed with expert methodology. With renewed optimism, I told the medic not to cut my shoe off. It was unlaced. They pulled the sock off. And there it was, all flat and gray and cold. I summed up a little courage and told my toes to move.

They did.

Love and The Great Outdoors

WHEN I WAS YOUNGER, I thought that finding the right person meant meeting someone who didn't live with their mother and had an equal appreciation for David Bowie. It wasn't until much later I realized most men fond of Ziggy Stardust probably weren't straight anyway, which has for the most part explained why I am still single.

Over the years, I've refined my criteria slightly to include anyone who can ride a mountain bike and owns a climbing rack with more economic value than their car. You'd think if I showed up at any old crag, the place would be teeming with dateable candidates. You'd think that by sundown, I'd be gnawing on some beef jerky over the romantic light of a camp stove with a tanned man named Taz who had just returned from a stint with the Peace Corps setting new routes in Patagonia.

The reality is that the statistical likelihood that you'll meet your next date in the outdoors is about as high as the likelihood that Cupid actually impales you with an arrow.

Most social interaction on the trail is done in the form of a wave and trying to hear over Paul Simon blaring in your headphones. (Okay, maybe I'm still single because I run to my mom's music. In my defense, *Graceland* is a great trail soundtrack.) We're either narrowly escaping a head-on collision on the bikes or under 14 layers of androgynous, sound-muffling ski gear.

This leaves us with few options. We can hang out at the

climbing gym with the hipsters and poach their dates; or we can get into the wrong tent at base camp.

There is, of course, the option of finding someone on the great interweb of possibilities. I'm less versed in this form of fated love. Once, I posted in an online forum looking for someone to mountain bike with and got about 17,000 responses from men who motocross while chugging Pabst. I could maybe deal with the motocross.

The reality is, the older we get and the more set in our ways (hobbies that take over our lives and pocketbooks), the less flexible we become about what we want to do and who we want to date. Aside from the fact that it would be nice if they had an employee discount at Mountain Gear, we'd also like them to like all our favorite sports with equal fervor. I mean, really, if I met a guy into curling, would I give him my number?

Recently, I decided to make a list of the things I'd want in my life and things I did not want in my life. It went something like this:

Must have:
1. Coffee
2. Laughter
3. Adventure

Don't want:
1. Gluten
2. Asshats
3. Laziness

This was because my previous list describing my dream partner was four pages dedicated mostly to a description of bike parts and bedroom tricks. I figured some simplification was necessary, and dare I say, an opening of my mind. I went back outside to observe all the single people complaining that they don't meet other single people, and I made a couple of observations.

First of all, we have to put our damn phones down. We need to take our headphones off. We need to come out of our isolating stimuli, take a giant leap of social faith, and make *eye contact*. And if we're feeling particularly outgoing, perhaps even start a conversation. I see a lot of head nodding and a lot of hey-how's-it-going, but I don't see people taking a moment to pause and interact on a human level.

Next, we need to try new things. Sure, I have my sports of choice (pretty much anything that is likely to cause an injury costing more than my insurance deductible), but how often am I willing to take time out of my stubborn priorities and play at something I likely suck at? It just so happens, plenty of really nice people are into curling, and a great number of them are probably even gluten-free. Stand Up Paddling might be a stretch though.

Opening your mind and your mouth is conducive to all sorts of wonders, like making new friends, discovering new muscle groups, finding new climbing partners, and maybe even meeting that person you're willing to share your last Clif Bar with. So the next time you go out, turn off your music, try something new, and say hello.

Extreme Gardening Could Be the New Fitness Craze

THERE'S BEEN A GROWING TREND in cross-training and sports that involves all kinds of athletic feats that both amaze and confound me. That being said, I seem to challenge my motor skills by merely setting one foot in front of the other without causing some sort of cataclysmic catastrophe.

Thus, it behooves me and my pride to not attend Pilates, Zumba, or Acro-Yoga until I've developed some basic gross motor skills to at least reduce the likelihood of public embarrassment. For this reason, and because food is involved, I put a garden in my yard. And because once I was checking out this lady's biceps at the store and said "CrossFit?" and she said "landscaper." Remember when everyone wanted Michelle Obama arms? There's got to be a correlation between that and her White House garden.

I started this year's training regimen by having a load of soil dropped off in a ridiculously inconvenient location in my yard: on my front lawn about two feet from the garden. This would normally be fine except there was a six-foot-high fence between the lawn and garden. The direct route was down some stairs, over the strawberry patch, around the fire pit, past the red ant torture mound, and to the other side.

Which brings us to the infinite possibilities of yard work for outdoor fitness. Yard work does not have a 6 a.m. step class that lasts an hour. It has a dynamic and ceaseless task list that is never, ever, ever ending. Moving the dirt meant moving the fence which meant using a lot more muscles and swear words than I typically do on a Sunday morning. By the end of my dirt-moving class, I was sure I'd be on the next "Strong is the new Skinny" poster.

Only, I didn't have time for that because while I was moving the dirt, I recognized the desperate need for weeding in the strawberry beds. I spent the next hour on my hands and knees doing some sort of Jane Fonda routine, except I was wearing wellies instead of spandex.

By then it was time for some electrolyte hydration in the form of lemonade (sports drink of choice by the American Society for Gardening Fitness). Proper hydration is key to yard-training success. Some athletes may prefer beer, but last time I tested this method I ended up growing flowers in the garden and tomatoes on the lawn.

Weeding the strawberry patch also meant discovering a new population of rocks (which breed like rabbits, apparently) that needed relocation. And so the day continued: moving rocks, pushing wheelbarrows, pulling roots, climbing stairs, swatting flies, and breaking a sweat in the sunshine.

By the end of the day, I felt like I'd run a marathon on all fours while pulling a plow. I flopped into a chair on the porch in a pile of dirt and grit and worm waste, exhausted.

So the next time someone invites you to join a CrossFit class, I recommend seeing if they'll pay you to come work in your yard instead. You can play some dubstep music and throw a few muscle-ups in there for authenticity.

Outside, your gym is everywhere.

Personal Challenge Replaces
Pistol Dueling

I'M NOT QUITE SURE HOW THESE THINGS HAPPEN, but they always seem to start with the formulation of Really Bad Idea No. 397 or No.14. One would think that by now I'd have learned to ignore any thought that is prefaced with:

Maybe I should . . .

or

Maybe I could . . .

Almost always, both of these end with an epilogue of PTSD therapy or, at the very least, chafing that would bring a grown man to his knees.

Recently, in a conversation surrounding the consideration of my most current Very Bad Idea, a friend noted that I was in a fetal position for most of the discussion. This leads me to believe that somewhere on a subconscious level I am quite aware of the misery I intend on embracing.

"That's just crazy," my big brother said. Because when brothers stop shoving hot peppers into your nose, they find other ways to abuse you. Like using reverse psychology to encourage your Very Bad Ideas.

From the formulation of the idea until the point of commitment, there is usually about a 37-minute window in which I glorify everything about it. Then I replace the term "Very Bad Idea" with "Challenge" because it draws much more public support.

Thus, determining that pushing oneself to the point of tears is healthy, I attempt to run around a mountain or in this case, sign up for Spokane's very own 24-hour Round the Clock mountain bike race. (Solo, because why not?)

While out training for what may qualify as my Worst Idea Yet, and in an attempt to turn my rear end into tanned leather before race day, I began exploring this idea of challenge.

Webster's says to challenge is to call or take part in a competition, typically a duel, and typically to prove something. So why is it that we as humans repetitively challenge ourselves? Was it always in our nature, or are we just replacing pistol duels with new hobbies?

Based on infinite historical quotes by JFK and the like, it would appear that challenge precedes personal growth and some sort of mysterious spiritual knowledge of self. By this logic, I should be nearly as enlightened as the Dalai Lama by now. As should anyone else who has suffered through a marathon or *Ishtar*.

The idea of self-challenge is that of leaving the comfort zone. And let's face it, Readers, we all live in a pretty bubble-wrapped comfort zone. Leaving it can bring us to new places, whether they are of self-awareness or mountain views or sobbing next to our bike on the trail. To challenge ourselves is to commit to a new kind of journey. Sometimes it means just changing your morning walk route. Sometimes it means climbing a mountain. And always it results in something undiscovered. It is what keeps our seemingly routine lives fresh and rewarding.

So if you haven't had a Very Bad Idea lately, take some time to ponder the infinite possibilities of discovery. You might just find yourself capable of something you never imagined. Your curiosity may just unveil the limitless potential of your world. You may just want to stock up on chafe balm first.

Maybe you could . . .

Precocious Child Forgets About Disneyland, Learns to Love Outdoors

I AM UNSURE WHETHER MY CHILD got really lucky with me as a mother, or if she's paying off some bad karma from a previous life. Better parents probably take their kids to Disneyland or something for spring break.

Not us.

Our spring break shenanigans would not be complete if we did not pack two weeks with camping in the rain, traumatizing exposure to roadkill, and at least one visit to a maritime museum dedicated mostly to anchors and limericks. Kids love that stuff.

Thus, we embarked on yet another of our adjusted family misadventures this spring, car packed with bikes, camping gear, climbing kit, running shoes, no less than forty pounds of cured meats and nuts, one mother, one sidekick, and one slightly less enthralled seven-year-old.

Just as I resisted having fun while growing up, my own daughter resisted having fun. I'm not sure what sort of genetic mutation we're passing down (no doubt the Viking blood is to blame), but in our family, 'fun' and 'extended misery followed by food' are interchangeable terms.

We began our trip by experiencing coastal monsoon climates from the comfort of our tent. Occasionally, the rain would pause to regain its momentum, and we would launch ourselves from the pile of sleeping bags to explore the soggy world around us. Usually by hiking the equivalent of the PCT in a single afternoon. Because kids also love hiking and making smart comparisons to the Trail of

Tears. (Parents: This is an opportune moment for a history lecture and blatant reality check that no matter how rough they think they have it, at least their dad isn't Andrew Jackson. Kids love history too.)

Now I have heard, probably from my own parents – an arguably unreliable resource at best – that if you continue to expose your children to these sorts of explorations of the world, they will one day enjoy them. Possibly not until they've grown up, paid for a lot of therapy, and had their own children.

Honestly, I don't know what is not to like about spooning oatmeal into your face from a half-washed camp cup while you shiver in the morning sunrise.

"Isn't this invigorating?!" I exclaim as I fish a pine needle out of my coffee.

"*Normal* families go to Disneyland for spring break, Mom."

"Yeah, but we had a *real* mouse in our tent this morning! That's way more authentic than Mickey."

By the end of the first week, she had stopped mapping out the mileage to a theme park detour and begun making her peace with our journey. And then something amazing happened . . .

It began with an adventure across the sand dunes, in which she leapt and ran and rolled with the playfulness of a carefree child. It was undeniable. She was having fun.

On the last day of our traipsing through the wonders of nature, seven years of schlepping my kid along were justified in a single episode of incomparable parenting pride.

My educated-but-uninterested daughter tied a figure eight knot into her climbing harness (thus far used mostly as an outdoor accessory) and told me she was going to climb to the top of the route we'd just set up. On the cliffs of Smith Rock. And then she did.

"I can see all the mountains from up here!" she yelled down to me as I stood jaw agape, heart swelling.

I don't know a lot about the Matterhorn, but I can tell you that dangling from a single rope a couple hundred feet up a canyon offers equal adrenaline and has a way better view. And chances are, we both built a little character along the way.

An Oasis in Name Only

I WENT TO ARIZONA LAST WEEKEND to visit friends only to discover that in November, Arizona is 90 degrees blanketed with blue skies. There were palm trees. And cacti. And every house had a swimming pool.

Apparently, my sheltered, backwoods living has kept me blind to this reality, although I have friends that 'travel south' for the winter. I figured it was a sort of Chopin migration, something to alleviate their asthma perhaps. I did not realize it was an oasis of glorious weather. I wondered, for a brief moment, why everyone did not live in the desert paradise.

So, on a beautiful Saturday (like every other Saturday in Arizona, I assume), I ventured outside, having not yet seen anything but the route from the airport. I hit a wall of warm air as I stepped out the door and pitter-pattered my way down the street. I quickly realized that staying hydrated in the desert is rather a full-time job. I made my way toward a park. Surely, it was a gateway to some trail or scenery.

I passed dozens of houses and manicured yards. They all looked exactly the same. The yards had no lawns or usable space – just gravel and palm trees. I saw no toys, no bikes, no signs of human presence other than the blatant urban sprawl. I saw perfectly shiny and unused pickup trucks and wondered why one would spend a small fortune on a vehicle they could not really use. I ran past home after home and did not once see nor hear children. On a *Saturday*.

I ran to the park – one that was surely planned in the initial design of the entire suburb: a swath of desert land converted into floral pattern of streets and 3 bed, 2 bath homes. The park, perfectly manicured like the sidewalks, streets, and yards, was empty.

I ran through the park, across the neighborhood to another park. It, too, was empty. I ran to the edge of the trendy-named estates, to where streets were built but no homes yet, and watched a police car hurriedly drive in and out of the side streets.

I wondered if someone had reported a runner. Maybe it wasn't allowed in this neighborhood. I had accidentally kicked a piece of gravel onto the pavement and failed to put it back. It was the only thing out of place I'd seen in two miles.

I ran to where the humans had stopped their takeover of the sands. A perfect straight line of roadway and broad gutters for flash floods. Civilization ended in an abrupt cliff of development. In front of me extended nothing but desert, jagged rocks, and in the distance, violent red-brown mountains. They were the most hopeful form of resistance I could see.

I stopped and looked into the quiet. The warm wind blew my hair into my face and reminded me of how parched I was. What was out there? Was it more alive than the silent brown stucco boxes stacked together?

I turned and ran back to my friend's home in the same silence and solitude.

"Do you go hike in those mountains?" I asked when I got back.

"No, those are on the reservation," they said.

When I flew back into Spokane, it was 41 degrees and raining. I drove through town and saw runners, soggy children, people walking their dogs. I saw yards being used (sometimes as dumpsters, but still) and people interacting. I saw homeless people in trash bags. I saw all the colors and all the shades of humanity displayed in their raw beauty.

I came home and put on my running shoes, desperate for the antidote to what I had seen. I found it in the trees, in the muddy runners that passed me, in the deer that crossed my path.

The oasis, my friends, is here.

When History Repeats Itself

BACK IN 1985, my youthful and blissfully unaware parents had this fantastic idea that they could move back to the land. They would lead a simple life with their children, grow their own food, cut down the wood to build their own house, and be free from the oppressive battle of being an American grownup.

Boy were they wrong.

It turns out, living off the land is really hard work that takes a moderate amount of skill. Mind you, this was before YouTube, where you can now achieve master craftsmanship skills in a two-minute video. They had to read books and, well, make a lot of mistakes.

I don't remember their suffering or stress as much as I have vague memories of my dad freaking out because we forgot to start the generator. Or that time my mom nearly blew up the inverter trying to make espresso (we were sophisticated hippies). I remember stacking a lot of wood, shoveling a lot of snow, and hiking the two-mile driveway with a sled full of laundry.

These things were a way of life. I don't recall thinking our family was particularly different from any other family. Except we got really excited when all five of us crammed into a motel room for the night and watched a TV. And we had never even really heard of camping because most summers my bedroom was a tent.

It wasn't until I was nine and went to a public school that I discovered there were other ways of living. I also discovered New Kids on the Block and was rather disappointed that no one knew Led Zeppelin, Pink Floyd, or David Bowie.

This was the beginning of an era of resistance. Why couldn't we have a telephone? Or indoor plumbing? How come my parents moved to the woods anyway? You know, in *other* people's homes they just turn a switch and it gets warm. Those kids don't have to do nearly as many chores as I do. What kind of torturous childhood is this anyway?

I vowed to move to the city as soon as I had my freedom. I would never chop wood again. The water pump would never freeze. The lights would never dim.

I experienced all that for the last twenty years. Modern amenities and urban living. Turns out, I kinda like chopping wood. And it's cheaper than CrossFit. Thus, in my romantic nostalgia of off-grid homestead memories, I did a crazy thing this week.

I bought a house.

On ten acres.

Off-grid.

And just like my parents, I am already making all kinds of ridiculous rookie mistakes. Like deciding to move in the middle of winter to a home that has: a) no supply of firewood and b) questionable access during snow season. Because if you're going to do something hard, why not make it almost impossibly hard?

This is the beginning of a new adventure in crazy. One that I will schlepp my entire family through because somewhere rooted deep in my core belief system is the idea that hardship makes for strong character.

Also, I am naively clinging to the idea that it isn't that hard. If only because I have many more resources than my parents had. Like YouTube and *The Idiot's Guide to Solar Powered Homes*. And, of course, my parents. Something tells me they now know a thing or two about moving back to the land.

Off-Grid Living: How to Feel Like You Are Camping Year Round

DETERMINED TO EXPERIENCE THE GLORIES OF HOMEOWNERSHIP, I spent my first night at the new and still unnamed cabin/ranch/lodge/casa. I have been feverishly thinking about what to call the place because it feels rather like an orphaned baby right now, only more needy.

I read a blog on "How to name your farm or ranch or homestead" that had a lot of advice on identifying qualities and characteristics of said new home. They picked things like "leaning birch" and "barn kitten hatchery" then included them in some sort of charming name.

With this in mind, I hauled a weekend's worth of living supplies up the hill: fourteen down comforters, enough food for eight days (which will last my kid until about 3 p.m. after which point she'll have to go rabbit hunting for sustenance), a number of tools that look useful but I cannot identify by name, and coffee.

For the record, this is approximately what I carry in my Search and Rescue pack, though I try to leave room for an avalanche probe and shovel.

I figured that in 48 hours I should be able to experience the 'feel' of the place. It would speak to me, and like gospel being sung from heavenly angels, the Truth would pour forth from my lips.

But the pipes were frozen in the kitchen, and I'm pretty sure angels don't swear. Also, it is hard to get signs made with all those ?!#%!& characters in them. If you name a place, it has to have a sign or it doesn't count.

I have been emotionally prepared for freezing pipes all along. I grew up with freezing pipes, and though I do not remember the inconvenience of wet rag baths, I do recall the cursing tirades of my father. You could hear him through the floorboards as he crawled under the house to criticize the plumber who had left pipes exposed (also known as Dad, since he built the place himself).

Heating frozen pipes in a straw bale house is like trying to gently coax a woman to go into labor. Some mix of unknown things must occur in the right order, then she'll go when she damn well pleases, and you better be ready. Also, it apparently may take nine months. By late June, I'm expecting to have water in the kitchen again.

Undeterred by this minor inconvenience, I was thrilled to see that turning my bathroom into an equatorial climate with a propane heater *did* actually thaw the pipes there, and the shower came exploding to life. This was celebrated by cleaning the spiders out of the tub, only to discover it was not draining. Apparently, the drain is frozen too.

I comforted myself with the knowledge that I could at least have warm water to wash dishes in the bathroom sink. And the toilet flushed. Having grown up with an outhouse positioned approximately a half day's hike from the house, indoor plumbing still feels like rather a luxury.

As the house heated, I did things one does in backwoods living. I chopped kindling, which retained a sort of productive quaintness and was easier than chopping firewood. I was so pleased with my kindling-making skills, I accumulated quite the stockpile only to realize the fire was going out. Then I burned most of the kindling trying to get it going again.

The house warming inspired a hatching of bugs that turned the upstairs into a sort of Valhalla for lizards. In fact, I considered getting one just to keep the stink bug population down. Stink bugs are sneaky little things. I can clear the premises of them, and by the time I've put the vacuum away, there are another dozen marching slowly toward my bed.

I know this is the goal of the stink bug nation: To silently persevere toward me while I am sleeping so I will wake up with hundreds of them waving their creepy little tentacles at me in a slow-motion attack.

I did not sleep that first night.

In the morning, my person brought my first-cup-of-morning-coffee-in-the-new-house to me in bed. No bugs were on me, but I could see a few in the corner waiting for me to forget their presence. I vacuumed them up. More appeared. I feared the army accumulating in my vacuum was plotting their escape while surviving on dead houseflies. I envisioned them with tiny maps and tiny military hats and one especially stinky general. I plugged the tube with a paper towel just in case.

Tired but determined, I worked on house things. At least I had warm water in the bathroom and a stove to heat my coffee.

Then the propane ran out. I washed dishes in cold water in a shallow bathroom sink. I warmed my coffee on the wood stove. I went out to change the tanks, but I didn't have the unidentifiable tool I needed to do this.

Defeated, I sat next to the wood stove with my coffee and wondered if it was time to return to the city where my house warmed at the turn of a knob.

Outside, I saw B stacking snow cubes. She had been out there for hours gathering miscellaneous pieces of discarded junk to employ in the construction of a snow fortress. I noted she did not have a bug problem. She appeared so industrious and pleased.

I remembered why we had begun this new adventure in the first place, grabbed my vacuum, and got back to work. Because no matter what, I am not naming this place Pine Beetle Lodge.

Preserving Sledding Heritage Through the Generations

"I DON'T THINK THIS IS A GOOD IDEA," said B staring down the abyss of our new driveway.

It is the kind of driveway that, when you buy it, you also buy yourself a set of good chains and accept the reality that you'll be using them most of the winter.

It is also the kind of driveway that makes you think about its tobogganing potential – even before you think of practical things like being able to drive it. For what use is a driveway if it does not serve several purposes?

This driveway is the stuff of sledding legends yet to be made. And most likely a few trips to the urgent care center, honestly. Standing at the top of it, we watched the narrow road hug the hillside as it made a straight shot down, then disappeared into a right curve.

In my head, I remembered the bump there from driving up. We could probably catch a little air, and if landed correctly, just narrowly miss a head-on collision with the ponderosa in the bend, only to be catapulted around the corner at high speed for the next steep section.

Sledding down it at least had to be more fun than trying to drive up it.

"That's exactly why we need to try it, B, to find out how much of a good/bad idea it is,' I said as I flopped down our hot pink plastic toboggan and gestured like a welcoming airline stewardess to please step aboard.

"Keep all hands and feet inside the vehicle at all times. If you feel the need to pray, please do so quietly so as not to distract the pilot."

To understand the anatomy of my poor decision making, I would like to take a moment to analyze the evidence in Exhibit A – Photograph of Midstokke Clan Sledding, circa 1987:

- That is my father in full motorcycle race gear. Note the icy road and the metal runner sled. On this day, he said he went so fast, he briefly sledded into the future to see the Vikings win a football game. This is how we knew he was lying.
- Notice I am missing my two front teeth. They may have still been there before I started sledding.
- Notice also that, despite all claims by my parents that middle child syndrome is unfounded, the middle child is the *only* person in this photo who was not provided with a helmet.
- I was, however, provided with a can of Cheese Pringles as a trophy for not cracking my skull. Having no teeth, I had to suck on them until they were soft enough to swallow. But they were Pringles and the child equivalent of Nirvana, so it was fine.

B made one last stand with a solid I-don't-want-to, but we were already loaded in the sled and ready for launch. Before she had the chance to escape from an emergency exit, I had pushed off with surprising force and gained enough momentum to make any bail attempt risky at best.

This is good parenting at its finest.

The toboggan shot down the driveway, gaining speed as we tried to avoid careening over the hillside and disappearing into the gully. Between screams of terror/joy (it's hard to tell the difference at Mach 7), I could hear B warning me that we were going too fast. But it was too late to change that. I was not going to sacrifice a limb to slow down.

As the corner approached, we aimed with sheer will for the inside, leaning as much as we could without tipping, B still shrieking in horror/ecstasy as we snapped around, only to realize the hill drops at an even steeper angle before that bump, guaranteeing a launch worthy of Olympic ski jumping.

My mad laughter echoed through the snow-laden trees as we whooshed by at insane speeds. The only other sound was the toboggan rushing over snow with the rickety shake of a plastic roller coaster. B had either given up or decided to take in the beauty of our run with silent reverence.

A quarter mile later, tears and grins frozen on our faces, the sled came to a safe stop in the middle of the road. All riders and bodies were miraculously still intact.

"We should be wearing helmets," said B, the apparent voice of reason in our family.

"Yeah! Let's go get some and go again!" I said.

I noted an unusual craving for Pringles and a lower insurance deductible.

Coexisting with Nature in Your Kitchen

THERE ARE CERTAIN PEOPLE OUT THERE, I am sure, that have a sort of karmic magnet for chaos. They are the people that somehow manage to pile several catastrophes into a day and casually cook dinner on the side. I watch them from a distance and silently judge their sixth sense for disaster and mayhem.

Until now. In a single day last week, I managed to have a chimney fire *and* a water heater failure (the latter turning my straw bale walls into a sponge for giants) within hours of each other.

After I had disassembled and reassembled the entire chimney pipe and discovered a stink bug village, a wasp nest the size of my head, and conversed with most of the fire department (who now know me on a first name basis), the wall started spewing mud and hay. This isn't really what you want to see your new house doing, and though this is my first home, I was under the impression that water is supposed to stay in pipes for best results.

The next day, as I was cooking dinner and perusing my homeowner's insurance policy, I discovered the evidence of mice near my oven. Suddenly, other evidence made sense, and I realized the mice were likely making a time share out of my oven. Also, that unique flavor of my home-cooked sweet potato fries was probably hantavirus.

As my pipe-assembly tools were still handy, I took apart my oven to find the swankest mouse nest I've ever laid eyes upon. Cozy and warm, made from stove insulation, it was clear they had been having orgies under my burners while I made pancakes. It took me hours to clean out, and I'm pretty sure the little buggers moved back in the next day. I'm thinking I should just install a tiny toilet for them and put out a tiny doormat to make them feel at home.

I have been catching them in a live trap because I clearly have a soft spot. I believe the mice have taken to considering these live traps – Holds Up to 30 Mice!! – as sort of teen community centers. They do not seem at all disturbed when I peer in at their fat little bodies as they continue to munch away at apples and nuts left for them. Perhaps I need to install a tiny pool table in there.

It would appear that mice and stink bugs and wasps have been here much longer than my house, having established themselves as permanent residents of the land and structures upon it. I'm hoping there is a way we can co-exist, preferably with me *inside* the building and those creatures *outside*.

Until then, I will continue to verbally threaten them whenever I go into my pantry. "Remember that guy on *Never Cry Wolf*?!" I shout as I open drawers and cabinets, prepared for them to leap out at me.

I think they know what a carnivorous coward I am and rather take delight in my generosity of releasing them back into the wild. I imagine a steady stream of them are making a pilgrimage through the forest and straight back to my house.

I'm going to need more traps. And some doll furniture.

The Road Less Traveled Leads to Good Neighbors

I RECENTLY MOVED INTO THE COUNTRYSIDE. Although this term suggests something of rolling hills and sprawling farms, in the Panhandle it means Backwoods Idaho. Also known as the birthplace of national adventures like Ruby Ridge and preppers. Like many pockets of the rural Northwest, it is full of good forest and good people.

It is also the home of roads that thaw in a phenomenon of 'spring breakup' that flatlanders struggle to comprehend. I know this because the first day there was a trickle and a pothole in the road, my Kentucky boyfriend came home to dramatically report the destruction of the entire route and declare breakup had arrived.

"Did you lose any children or vehicles into this so-called chasm of mud?" I asked.

He blinked at me.

"Then it's not breakup yet. Tether the children and just wait."

A week later, when the rain had worked its magic of bog creation, he half-buried his jeep on the way home. If you can still open the doors, the situation is not dire, and one should merely drop a few trees on which to crawl out. Or one can wander over to the neighbor's house to see if any of their vehicles have survived the appetite of the earth.

The neighbor came more as emotional support than anything else. Various rigs and ropes were assessed for effective problem resolution. They too were consumed by the vortex of muck.

(NASA scientists may want to study this plasma substance as some localized form of a black hole or portal to a parallel universe.)

There was humming and hawing and a great deal of cussing and some chuffing too. The men did man things. As far as I can tell, that basically means having complex conversations of profound communicative understanding without actually *saying* a word. Friendships were formed. Trucks were retrieved.

Days later, we found four enormous pig carcasses on our property. I would have understood if they had been used to fill the veritable swamp of my driveway. Instead, they had been tossed in the draw – a steep tree and weed overgrown embankment that leads to a fresh water source. Despite a ripe coyote population, I suspect that this is not the best place for decomposing livestock.

Now, swine are a stubborn animal, both alive and dead. I know this because my mom has one of those pocket pigs people 'domesticate' and train to be an indoor bully of humans and other house pets. She named her Violet because Charlotte was too cliché and Bacon was too blatant.

Pigs are supposed to be very smart and uniquely trainable, but my experience is that they fall on the spectrum of personality disorders somewhere between narcissist and sociopath. "Look at her setting boundaries," my mom will sweetly note as the pig tries to chomp through the bones on my ankle like I'm in a bad mafia movie.

The pigs in my canyon were a great deal larger and a great deal more grotesque, of course, and they urgently needed relocating. Kentucky called on our other neighbor (driveway to the left versus driveway to the right). A system of ropes and pulleys and tractors was implemented. There was cussing and chuffing and some nose holding.

Only a really good neighbor would subject themselves to the carnage witnessed that day. I should probably bake them some cookies. A bacon casserole may raise eyebrows. The men bonded, likely over the trauma-inducing nature of the experience. Again, friendships were formed.

In the city, our over-busy, over-stimulated lives combined with a strange culture of independence and isolation kept our neighbor relationships superficial. There was a ladder lending here and a 'good day' there. And once, for a couple of months, we mostly had to communicate through the police we asked to swing by for a drunken brawl. (We would sit in bed with popcorn and peer through our blinds.)

At first, I was concerned the neighbors would be wary of us because I put up a hand-painted mailbox with rainbows. To avoid being labeled as liberal hippies and maintain a level of conservative respect, we occasionally shoot guns at things. Mostly the woodpecker that finds his breakfast at sunrise in the siding directly behind my bed.

As we settle into our new surroundings, we have forged entirely new relationships of community, kindness, and even need. They are friendships created out of generous acts, good humans, and a fair bit of commiserating. They have grit and substance and shared memories.

Yet when we plant our roots, buy homes, or sign rental contracts we can't leave, neighbors are often some of the longest lasting relationships we have. And heaven knows they bear witness to our lives more than many of our other friends. The happenstance interactions do not allow us to determine what we present (fetching the paper in a bathrobe at best). There is a raw, sweet humanity to this different kind of intimacy. A friendship of chance and time.

In Robert Frost's "The Mending Wall," he says, "Good fences make good neighbors." It wasn't until recently I realized it was the mending that made the good neighbor, for the fence was not a barrier but a common ground.

Beauty of Nature Indisputable – Sometimes

WHEN I MOVED BACK INTO THE WOODS, I had this impression that I would be traipsing around the wilderness in a flowing dress, singing old Disney tunes while birds and squirrels perched on my arms. I thought that moving into nature demanded a sort of meshing with the animal kingdom – the kind where the deer visit, and you name the domesticated family of raccoons that live under your porch. Instead, I find myself fantasizing about creative ways to destroy critters one at a time.

In the beginning, I considered it my rookie backwoods skills. I must have failed to seal off the house appropriately and mice were getting in. I ought to catch them and put them back in the forest where they belong. It only took a short while before I realized the mouse nation was making a methodical and coordinated effort to conquer my home and claim it as their own country. I snap their necks now.

The woodpecker I thought was just helping me get rid of my stink bug problem. "Look how amazing it is that nature keeps all things in balance," said my naive city girl brain. Until the sunrise jackhammer noise drilled a hole the size of a baseball in the most inaccessible part of my third-floor exterior.

A few BB gun pellets, and we had an understanding. Maybe that's all it would take: I needed to set boundaries with the animals so they could go do their animal things at a safe distance from my house.

Now there is a family of squirrels living in the wall of my third floor. The woodpecker managed to make a gorgeous room-with-a-view suite for them including a French door entrance and spacious south-east facing windows for excellent morning light. There is plenty of pinecone storage space for year-round eating, and I think I may even occasionally hear a tiny little boudoir flushing.

Naive as I am, I had refused to put traps in my garden for whatever was eating my peas and chard. If I lived in the forest as an animal and found peas and chard, I'd munch them too. I reinforced my fencing and hammered those little peeping gopher deterrents into the ground. My spacious garden sounded like a video arcade until some other critter got tired of it and dug a series of trenches, tearing them out of the ground. Then it ate the last of my peas and chard.

Even my brown cow dog, who is only still alive because of her cuteness, chomped down my entire patch of Brussels sprouts and nearly a complete row of broccoli. It's like she is siding with *them.*

And at five AM this morning, as the sun began to creep over the hills, the daily squirrel brawl outside my window was all I could take. I think the squirrel family has a loose cannon, maybe a squirrel with anger management issues or squirrel Tourette's. He just sits in the tree a few feet away from my pillow and chatters like a psychotic, rabid, over-caffeinated varmint until my brain threatens to explode.

For the last hour and a half of my broken sleep, I have dreams in which I am a renegade exterminator, laughing madly with flamethrowers and rat poison, and all of nature runs screaming from my granite mountaintop like the animals from a forest fire. Behind me lays destruction as artillery explosions rise into the sky, my house unscathed, the wisteria in full bloom.

When I get up, cranky and tired, and wander downstairs for coffee, the squirrel stops chattering, and there is a hummingbird stuck in my window. I reach out, cup him in my hand, and take him onto the deck to fly away.

But he doesn't. He just sits there in my palm, sipping nectar from the flowers while I sip my coffee. A half hour later, he takes flight. Maybe I shouldn't have started singing.

Coping Mechanisms for Unexpected Disasters

I AM STANDING IN MY KITCHEN CRYING. There are very few records of actual Midstokke crying to date, but this was the real deal. Full-fledged, trembling lip, snotty nose crying.

My dad is wearing a tool belt and a pair of noise muffs over his already deaf ears. He tries to help and says, "Maybe we should remodel your bathroom another time."

My choked tears turn into a full sob. I want to do laundry in my own house.

I've just come back from the well-drilling guy. Everything had been going fine until I planted a garden. In fact, I planted a hallelujah garden with a pack of friends on my birthday, a garden that will make the angels sing and be cause for legitimate harvest festivities. But then my hose stopped working. I don't know a lot about gardening except that water seems to be rather essential.

Here's a little piece of advice for my young readers: Stop going to college. All my regurgitated MBA knowledge was relatively useless as this debacle unfolded. Buy a drill instead.

I get a sparky up to the house to check out my pump. My sparky wears a black utility kilt with wool socks and big, black boots. I like him because he speaks electrician in a way I understand. Sparky says the pump is working. The well might not be.

In the history of wells, barring a few biblical references to undeserving villages of idol worshippers, very few wells have gone dry.

I like to consider myself an exception to most rules.

While I will preach and prose much on the merits of self-reliance and back-to-the-land living, the reality is slightly different. If you want water, you either need to have a mattress stuffed with cash or marry a well-driller. I recommend the latter. I think they earn more than most Hollywood plastic surgeons, minus the liability suits.

On that note, if there are any eligible well-drillers in the area, please call me. I am tired of siphoning my quickly draining pond to water the garden with tadpoles, although I expect they make quite fine fertilizer.

I am in a daze as I sign the contract with the drilling company. Basically, they are going to poke a hole in my granite mountainside and see if they find water. They might not, though, but don't worry, I get to give them a lot of money anyway.

I'm signing papers as I wonder if my kid can put herself through college as a Vegas dancer. Then I remember college isn't helpful in these situations, and I'm grateful she is going to a hippie socialist school where they'll learn how to turn urine into water and sing fertility songs.

All the fine print says if they don't find water, ("But don't worry, I can drill 800 feet,") it's not their problem. I'm trying to calculate in my head silently while my stomach sinks. At $24.00 a foot, that is. . . at least *both* of my kidneys.

I'm trying not to cry. I'm thinking about how I have been climbing a ladder into my bedroom for weeks now, how all I want is the ability to wash my clothes in my own house.

"Yep, when we break ground, we call it 'sitting-in-the-hot-seat,'" he jokes as he hands me a copy of a paper that says he can put a lien on my land if I don't pay.

Advice for drilling companies: Please issue waterproof mascara, tissues, and hemorrhoid cream (for the puffy eyes, works like a charm) to your clients before you hand over your quotes. I made it back to my car and then my eyes started leaking.

I cried so much, I wondered if I could just pump *that* into my house. If I had expected to drill a well, it would have been different. This was not part of the plan. Stairs and a kitchen counter were.

I reminded myself that no one had died. Money is just money. Then I thought I better call my mom and ask if she was planning on giving me an inheritance, and if so, is she planning on dying soon (and having a budget funeral) or would she consider an advance. Maybe I can just move back in with her. I am showering and laundering at her house anyway.

My dad has sympathy in his eyes. We're tough Norwegians, but I guess that means we understand tears are an indication of being well beyond the breaking point.

"We'll get your bathroom in," he says. The mere thought of doing laundry in my own house soothes my soul. I take a deep breath. I need a reminder of why I thought this craziness was a good idea.

I find it on my deck staring out at the mountains. When this brief moment of overwhelming stress is a distant memory, the view will still be mine. Perspective can be so revealing.

Fetching Firewood and
Other Life Lessons

I DIDN'T KNOW IT GROWING UP, but some of the most valuable wisdom I would learn would come from chopping wood. Or rather, from having a wood-heated home that requires the acquisition of trees, appropriate sawing, hauling, piling, chopping, stacking, and so on. It is a process that requires both brawn and brains. And while no one has accused me of the latter, I have been mistaken for a rugby player or Latvian bear wrestler on more than one occasion.

As a child, firewood season was abhorred. This could have something to do with the fact that firewood hauling was also a form of Machiavellian punishment instilled by my parents (who are arguable geniuses). If my brother or I were the cause of some sort of behavioral infraction – such as trying to find out if chickens could swim, hiding and drinking all the JOLT! cola, or talking back – we would be ordered to 'fifty logs.'

Our firewood supply was a quarter mile away up a road that curved around our property, went over the creek, and dove into the steep side of the mountain where tamarack and pine had been felled and stacked earlier in the season. We would take our red, plastic toboggans strung with bailing cord, sling the rope around our waists, and trudge up the hill where we did our darndest to find the smallest rounds of firewood possible.

By July, we'd caused enough trouble that most of the small logs were gone. Earning fifty logs in late summer meant one could only get maybe six logs in a single, heavy load. Into the woods we'd go to load our sleds and drag them home. The tiny cord was drawn taut against our hips or shoulders, we leaned forward like Clydesdales and stomped one foot in front of the other, the sound of rock and dirt scraping under the plastic as we inched our way toward the house. Sadly, we knew no chain gang songs at the time, though we may have sung a bible camp song or two.

There was a time when my mother was building rock walls around everything, and we had to fetch rocks instead of wood. Although optimistic to begin with, I soon discovered that rocks are no lighter than firewood. Surprisingly, while I was learning a lot about weight distribution, torque versus speed, and geology, I never learned how to stop getting in trouble.

Some decades later, I find myself smiling at a pile of log rounds on a Saturday morning. My person has fetched several trees and delivered them, like a sweet gift to his lover, to our back door. Many advancements have been made in the technology of firewood acquisition since my childhood: He used an ATV and trailer, and there was no punishment involved, just a desire to not freeze this winter.

I set to the work of setting up the rounds, lining up a selection of chopping tools (axes, mauls of different weights, a cup of coffee, and soundtrack). My palm wrapped around the wooden handle of the maul (we are becoming old friends), and I rolled my shoulders a few times. It is a big pile of wood. The rain is coming. I want it all split and stacked before the weekend is over.

Each piece of wood that splits has a different story, whether it is one of how frustrated I was with the many knots or how hot I think it may burn on a cold, winter day. For hours and hours, I swing, grunt, thud, split, toss, stack the wood. Tired and sore, I wake up the next day to do the same. I am elated as I see my woodshed fill one foot, one row at a time.

It smells like soil and splinters and hard work in there. I stand before the stacks and I can already feel the heat of the flame through the stove, hear the gentle clacking of my knitting needles, see my children huddled around the flickering light as the snow falls outside.

"Why do we even have to heat our house with *wood*?" asks my daughter as she complains bitterly at the prospect of manual labor (apparently an antiquated practice amongst the younger generations). She declares me a mad woman, much as I accused my own parents of breaking a number of internationally recognized child labor laws.

Yet somehow what was once a form of discipline has become one of my most rewarding experiences. My guess is my parents knew exactly what they were doing.

Running Away and Other
Outdoor Development Programs

AT THE RIPE OLD AGE OF SEVEN YEARS, having determined that I had the wisdom and acuity to identify injustice as well as the courage to stand up against it, I ran away. A line in the snow had to be drawn.

I had been outside on a wintry day peeling logs. The reds and browns of the bark made a carpet on the snow. Most of our living quarters were in fact *outside* because a family of five doesn't exactly fit well in a pickup truck camper, no matter how much you love each other.

There was room inside only to eat, write sentences (our current form of discipline/homeschooling, two-birds-with-one-stone kind of method), and sleep. Everything else about our lives was done in the snow and timber of our new 'home' – twenty-six acres of off-grid paradise for the optimistic and naive Californians we were.

Seeing as we were busy gathering moss for chinking and cutting down trees for our future log home, we were pretty well occupied with our outside activities. My jobs were to make sure my infant sister didn't roll off the cab loft bed, stir the beans, and peel logs. My recollection of labor hours may be skewed, but I'm pretty sure some international standards were broken.

On one such afternoon, feeling particularly aware of the task at hand, I tromped into the camper, presumably to warm my frozen fingers, kicking snow from my boots and closing the thin door behind me. The camper was warm and inviting (comparably – usually there was ice on the floor and burn marks on the ceiling).

Ahead of me, in the middle of the workday, stretched out on the expansive grown-up bed, lay my mother with her nose buried in a *trashy novel.* Probably Danielle Steele at that. There were breasts on the cover. That was all the incriminating evidence I needed. My little sister, not even a year old, was nestled to her chest, feeding happily in the oasis of sleeping bags, propane heat, and prose.

I'm not sure what I found most offensive. I slept in the cupboard above the kitchen table, so maybe I was incensed that I didn't have the same ability to stretch to my full length or hold a book more than four inches from my face. Most likely it was my lack of awareness: My mother was probably reading medical manuals to pass her midwifery exams while struggling to nurse my malnourished, adopted sister.

In any case, I took in that image of sloth and gluttony, seeing her sprawled out like a harem queen, a first wife, a Sorel-stomping enchantress, and revolted.

"What is this?" I inquired with vehemence. "How can you *lay* here wallowing in your inertia and lethargy [I was seven, I probably said 'laziness'] and order me to work outside in the cold all day like . . . like a *slave?!*"

If I recall correctly, she sort of chuckle-chortled. That's a half-laugh, half-cough, half-pause-so-child-can-run-before-inevitable-walloping. But I wasn't done yet.

"If I were not doing all this work, you would not survive. Clearly you do not appreciate me. I am running away."

Strangely, the conversation ended there. There were no protests, tears, no motherly sobbing or begging for mercy. No pleas for reconsideration or forgiveness. Just the quiet turning page of her cheap literature and the echo of her chortle.

True to my word and dedicated to my honorable fight against tyranny and oppression, I marched across the snowy creek and down the road. I wished I'd eaten lunch first.

Those sons of guns will see what sort of trouble they've gotten themselves into. Who's gonna peel their logs now, eh? They'll have to live in that camper forever!

Approximately 400 yards later, I imagined they'd had enough of a lesson. I just wanted them to *understand,* not necessarily be scarred or damaged. Also, it was cold, and I didn't know how to build a shelter, just a log house. So I walked back to the camper.

Surprisingly, nothing had changed. The world had not ended. It was like I hadn't even been gone. My mother was not in a panic trying to rouse a search party. In fact, she was merely turning the next page.

"I have returned," I said. "I forgive your ignorance and know that you'll try harder now."

Then I went back to my log peeling.

And yet I learned one of my most valuable outdoor skills that day: Don't wander too far because maybe no one is coming to find you. Also: Pack lunch.

Later that day, my writing career began in the most subtle of ways.

I will not run away until my chores are complete.

I will not run away until my chores are complete.

X 100.

The Slow Goodbyes We
Never Want to Say

"HOW LONG?"

"12-15 months," says Sarah.

Shawn got lost flying his plane. He went to the doctor. The doctor sent him to the ER. The ER sent him to surgery. The surgeon gave him a death sentence.

In a single moment, the fragility and impermanence of the world, not *The World*, but the little ones of our own we've made upon it, is thrust before us. Our ideas, hopes, our beliefs about being good people, recycling, and eating organic are wiped out, obliterated with the only inescapable truth there really is: We die.

I drive my car toward the Cascades, those mountains that Sarah and I explore together, where so many memories and misadventures have been made. Where plans for more of the same are concocted. The mountains look the same, but how can that be?

Since I've known the two, I have wanted to grow up to be like them. I want to be floating the Grand Canyon and telling campfire stories of that time *'we got so lost on a moped in Vietnam, we considered just living in the jungle for a few months until someone found us.'* The book of life they wrote together is filled with pages of camaraderie, brave and arguably insane travel, and the last time Sarah bailed Shawn out of jail.

That was 25 years ago. They haven't had a drink since.

They have climbed mountains in Nepal, though, and learned how to fly planes, and gone to Burning Man every year, and watched the solar eclipse. And they have upcycled and bicycled and spread the good word of preserving Our Mother. They have been true activists by setting the finest example.

My car drops a gear as I speed past Highway 97. Sarah and I ran the Enchantments loop in a day last summer. It was hotter than the front row of a strip club by afternoon and, tired of my slumbering pace, she took off ahead of me the last few miles. She left a note on my car. "Hitchhiked to my van." She had wanted to get home early enough to have a few hours with Shawn before the week started.

Come to think of it, every single mountain madness we'd ever survived, Sarah had a parking lot transition faster than a triathlete. Dump soggy gear, grab food and hold in face while changing shoes, say the goodbye-sorts-of-things while leaving rubber on the road as she shot back to her urban oasis and husband. *What will she rush to now?*

Shawn and I are going out for ice cream. It's raining, but neither we nor our dogs care. When death pulls your lotto number, ice cream guilt is absolved, and rain is just wet. We order ridiculously huge bowls and eat them slowly while sitting on bar stools, staring out at Seattle nightlife. Every time the door opens, cigarette smoke wafts past us. The dogs blink at us through the window.

"I got a ski pass to Snoqualmie," says Shawn.

If Shawn has led by example in how he has lived, he is going to do the same in how he dies. It gives me pause to wonder if living and dying are all that entirely different. Shawn would say that other than the Miralax, doctor appointments, and tragedy, they are not.

I cannot reconcile that the mountains are not sagging with the weight of this loss as I drive home again. I stop to stare at their emerald timber walls towering above my head. The wind is blowing cold and sharp, and my hair sweeps across my face. There is solace here, in that which was before us and will remain long after us. Perhaps they are impervious and graceful so that we must not be.

If our bodies must be left behind, our memories can continue on. Make many of them. The kind that make you laugh and cry, the kind that are triggered by smells and songs, those that are as big and real as the mountains. The kind that remind you of the saddest, most delicious bowl of ice cream you ever ate.

Rad Old People: The Only Real Age-Defying Pill

SOMETHING HAS CHANGED IN OUR AMERICAN culture of aging, deeming the process of aging a thing one ought to avoid despite its inevitability. In other cultures, we can still witness a sense of reverence and respect for the aging and elderly, a way in which the rites of passage that accompany only *time* are honored.

And then there's Botox. Where wrinkles are mitigated, collagen infused, breasts lifted, and testosterone injections promise a virility so potent, you'll be attracted to women with mustaches and cankles. We fear aging even more than disease (or we'd stop getting Botox and start eating salads).

Whenever I've been tainted by the culture of permanent youth – usually after grabbing a magazine at the hair salon – I panic about getting old. As you'll recall, I'm not quite forty, so this may seem silly. Thirty was a shock to me as well. It isn't just my mortality at stake here.

I stare at these women and think, *How many years have they consistently applied lotion and drank a gallon of water a day to make their skin look like that? Is it too late for me? Maybe if I start putting on lotion twice a day and drinking more water. Will I be happy if my skin appears nubile?*

I'm not sure if my male counterparts experience the same when grabbing the latest issue of *GQ*. Do you guys hope you'll go gray in that sexy salt-and-pepper way while maintaining sleek abs and climbing the corporate ladder? I think worrying about lotion might be better.

Whenever that realization of aging and the irreversible tick-tock of time starts freaking me out, I invite myself along with a group of people old enough to be my parents (or just my parents). I refer to them lovingly, perhaps a little patronizingly, as silver-sneakers, and then I get my ass handed to me.

There is nothing more humbling or inspiring than having someone twenty years your senior waste your huffing and puffing ego up a mountainside.

Last weekend, I got a double dose of it. I grabbed some running snowshoes and met with a few people on the cusp of retirement to climb up Schweitzer Mountain. There was a lot of gray hair happening. I thought I had it in the bag.

There I was, like a kid in the back seat, asking every quarter of a mile, "Are we getting close? We must be near the top now? How far is this round-trip?" I even forgot to pack my snack.

In addition to the joy of not getting lost (my usual mountain skill), my hosts imparted hours of invaluable wisdom upon me. All of them veteran long-distance runners, they had some passage rites I hope I never earn. I estimated that between the three of them, with their 50-milers and 100-milers and other such nonsense, they'd run a combined 18 billion or so miles.

I shamelessly asked every single rookie question I could between gasping for air. *How do I not bonk on a long race? What mistakes did you make? How do you avoid them now?* They all guided me with kindness and compassion. They shared the wisdom that only experience can offer. And I'm pretty sure none of them felt compelled to get Botox or airbrushed.

If this is aging, I'm not afraid anymore. If I can out-hike and out-run eager company, share stories, and contribute to others' journeys while I continue to explore my own, this is a path I can embrace with gratitude.

Mostly, I'm grateful for everyone who has patiently survived the aging process while tolerating the rest of us. I'm grateful for those of you clinging to your sharp minds or ski poles or mile times as a reminder to the rest of us that it isn't about the destination or how few wrinkles you have when you get there.

We need you. Don't give up on us. We'll catch up. In time.

The Inevitability of Extinction

"YOU'LL WANT TO GO ON SAFARI," says my mom, "before those animals are extinct."

The extinction we're currently trying to beat is Shawn's. He wants to climb Kilimanjaro before he wins that race with the animals of the savannah.

"Kilimanjaro?" I ask.

"Yeah, I've never been," he says.

I'm not particularly familiar with all the good ways to die, but I suspect it's just about the same as all the good ways to live. Ultimately, we spend our entire lives dying. We ask each other moot questions: *What would you do if you had a year to live?* Facing mortality, even from a distance, gives that question new perspective.

If that's the case, why am I so focused on the barn I need on my property? Having land and the tools to manage it without a structure in which to put them means I go through a lot of tarps. I do all the adult things to facilitate this barn planning: stashing money, getting quotes, drawing plans. I budget and I walk the land with the concrete guy, and we say really grown-up things about structural integrity.

I consider the future and how I can appropriately allocate my work hours to 'buckle down' and get through this project. As long as my blasted well doesn't dry up again, I should manage just fine if I work hard. When you are a homeowner, they say, you have to invest in your home. It's part of being a mature adult, long-term planning, bigger picture sort of talk.

Meanwhile, Shawn is dying. I'm planning a pole barn as if it is important while he plans his exit to the greater cosmos. Like Zorba, he laughs in the face of fate (and sometimes curses and cries at it). There was a line in that book about the difference between people who live like they are never going to die and people who live like they may die tomorrow.

The former put off their dreams and hopes, their reckless ideas, their passions, in the optimistic and perhaps naive assumption that there will be a tomorrow. They work hard and plan for that tomorrow with 401Ks and retirement savings and pole barns that 'increase the value of the property.' They put off the adventures. Sometimes they put off *living.*

They don't think that maybe the lions and giraffes are going to be gone by the time they shuffle the kids to college, retire, and head to Africa. They don't realize that rain forests, sequoias, the Great Barrier Reef, and icebergs are going extinct too. Or that it is impossible to make new memories when you're dead.

I really need to balance my books and look at barn plans, but I have a window of time to snowshoe up a mountain with a friend. I slap my laptop shut and head out for an epic journey into the snow-covered trees. Barn plans can wait until I get home.

We spend hours trudging through the snow, sharing laughter, tales of our sorrows, and a successful summit.

When I return home five hours later, face red and chapped, heart pounding, frozen smile and fatigue encompassing me, I see my dad has sent me some barn cost numbers. He says to budget for that but to leave a little room because it might cost more – it's good to have a buffer.

"Stick to the number," I say. "The buffer is going to Tanzania."

"Glad to see you've got your priorities right," he responds.

More Things We Never Recommend You Do

LET ME PREFACE THIS WEEK'S ADVENTURES with a very hearty *do-not-try-this-at-home.* Unless you have to. Then ignore the warnings.

I often speak to the importance and benefits of learning new things every day of our lives. It encourages mental growth, increases our sense of well-being, and even reduces brain atrophy. I did not realize exactly how much learning I would be doing this weekend.

It all began when my hot water heater exploded. Hot water heaters, I have decided, are somewhat resentful of their caged flows, their limitations, the way we humans can change their settings. Occasionally, one goes rogue, blows clean through a pipe, and tries to convince you it is Niagara Falls.

When your hot water heater is in your living room, this is inconvenient unless you happen to be standing in a five-gallon bucket and in dire need of a shower. I was neither.

When I grew up (in similar fashion), I remember watching my dad sulk and stomp around the house when life happened. Pipes froze. Generators needed oil changes. Dogs chased porcupines. Determined to accept the happenings of life as the odd additional chore here or there, I decided not to worry about the water heater.

I called seventeen plumbers to no avail, put a pot of water on the wood stove to heat, and dragged my rear end to the gym to "work out" just so I could take a shower. I thought, *Meh, people lived swell before showers anyway.* Then I patted myself on the back for being so calm and *mature* about it all.

I cranked up my wood stove, cozied up with the kid, and had enough hot water to do the dishes daily. Eventually, I hoped, a plumber would want to come over and install a new water heater. Unfortunately, the recent snowfall had my road almost impassable (unless you know how to chain up and white-knuckle your way up a mountainside in a trusty Subaru). There would be no service people headed my way until perhaps spring. They didn't seem too interested anyway.

By then, I'll be a handball and squash expert, a force on the treadmill, and playing bridge with the aquatic gymnastic team. If the gym had an espresso stand in there, I'd just move in under the stairs with a sleeping bag and a cardboard sign.

CAN'T PLUMB. WILL PLAY SQUASH FOR COFFEE.

But then I started detecting the earthy smell of smoke wafting through my rooms. I wasn't sure if I was getting a brain tumor or burning the wrong wood.

"Do you smell more smoke?" I asked my person.

"No," he said before he caught a plane across the country, far, far from impending disaster. It's like a sixth sense.

I let the fire go out and cleaned out the stove. I'd just scrubbed the pipe and burned one of those creosote logs weeks before. I started a new fire, chuffed by my proactive house-owner, responsibility-facing sort of work.

Smoke billowed from everywhere. The stove door. Every joint in the pipe. In an instant, the air was unbreathable, the house a cloud of black smoke. We shut the fire down, the smoke stopped. Now we had no hot water and no heat. It was dark, cold, and everything smelled like campfire. I lay in bed all night, wide-eyed, wondering how I would get onto my third-floor roof come daylight. There *had* to be a clog in the little silver thingy at the top of the other silver thingy.

I don't know a lot about wood stoves and chimneys. I don't know about extension ladders in snow piles or how to drill into the metal and make an anchor. But I do know that chimney sweepers don't work on Sundays, even if they *could* drive to my house. I also know how to climb.

I needed to get on that steep, metal roof somehow. I geared up, grabbed my rope and harness, and set to work. The snow piles from the roof were so big, I could easily hop onto the first floor. From there, I weighted the end of my rope, and after several failed attempts, launched it over the ridge and fed it to the ground. Right next to my trusty Subaru. The roof rack served as a beautiful anchor.

(Several concerned men subsequently noted the lack of reliability of a roof rack as an anchor. The rack was fine. I was never going to tax it with a fall because I had a double prusik system and a belay device, remaining in tension the entire time. To them I say: *Where the hell were you and your ladders?*)

Moments later, I was yanking the clogged spark arrester (the real name of the silver thing, apparently) off my stove pipe and *poof* *out came the billowing smoke!* Just like that, the problem was solved. The fire was stoked again. The pot of water got hot. I could do dishes. Almost all was restored once more. I whistled Chim-Chim-Cheroo for the rest of the day.

Now I just need to learn how to install an on-demand water heater. It has a lot of copper thingies on it. Someday I might figure out what they are called too.

Russians Shower Cold Too

BACK IN THE DAY, I lived in Germany and had a roommate from Estonia. Among teaching me how to make traditional Russian Borscht and other things, she also explained ad infinitum the benefits of conducting personal hygiene matters in frigid waters.

Because if someone gives you lemons . . . you take a cold shower in them.

It might appear that my column (and life) has become rather a soap opera with a focus on homesteading. It could only be made more interesting if I had some single lumberjack neighbors with moral autonomy, large biceps, and a smidgeon of plumbing experience.

My inbox filled with advice last week. Impressive, considerate, and helpful comments rolled in by people with far more knowledge and common sense than I have. I did notice a clear trend: Boys told me how I could have done it better/safer/differently. Girls told me I was rad and solution-oriented. I needed both varieties, so my heartfelt thanks goes out to each and every one of you.

Since then, I have conversed with no less than a dozen plumbers, people who know what PEX is, Bosch representatives, Takagi representatives, my dad, my dad again, then my dad some more. He's deaf, so he just blows up my phone with questions like, "How you like this mountain life now, eh?" I can't tell for sure, but I think there's a snicker in there.

What he doesn't know is that it will probably take me until his next visit to actually source the right supplies – just in time for him to install my new water heater. In May.

I received one letter this week that rather justifiably questioned my choice of a hard life, and I had to take a moment to ponder what may appear like misfortune. In my experience, true tragedy has a different taste. It's loss, broken hearts, and goodbyes we never had time to say. It is knowing our kids have grown up too fast while we worked too much. It is poverty, mass shootings, the death of thousands of endangered antelope, and every Vikings season.

After a plumbing company quoted me seven thousand, one hundred and forty dollars to replace my thousand-dollar water heater, I decided this, too, was an opportunity for learning. I did some reading like a grown-up, developed a network of friends, gyms, and family with hot water facilities, and ordered myself a swank new unit: 199,000 BTUs of boiling potential, baby!

If that weren't enough, I googled some things about PEX pipe and was thrilled to discover it comes in bright colors like red and blue. When girls do plumbing or buy cars, obviously the color heavily influences our purchase choices.

Projects around here are, simply put, not simple. I need to relocate the water heater so it is not quite so close to my delicate, straw bale walls. That requires propane adjustments, new venting, and some cautious planning. The most obvious place for my new infinite supply of gluttonous showers is my root cellar. My solar-fueled batteries live in there too. If you're unfamiliar with those, they off-gas a little hydrogen from time to time.

I'm not a chemist, but it seems like, one time, something bad happened when some smart people combined hydrogen and flames. And I'm not even smart, so I better be at least careful.

So yes, my dear readers. Stuff goes wrong all the time up here. It's good stuff though. Every time something blows up or melts or gets eaten by varmints, I have an incredible opportunity to learn something I know absolutely nothing about. I suppose it cuts a little into my free time, and some days I might prefer knitting. The fringe health benefits (purportedly: improved circulation, virility, vodka tolerance, and hacking skills) far outweigh the inconvenience.

Big Things, Little Things, and Perspective

I LOST A FRIEND TO SUICIDE THIS WEEK. It was the kind of shocking loss that leaves you confused and asking questions that may never be answered. It was the kind of loss that rips through a community, where heartache gives rise to unity, compassion, and grace.

It's 13 degrees outside in the shade, and every time I pass under a tree, I feel the bitter cold of this fickle winter seep beneath my soggy layers of wool. *Why do I even run on days like this? I'm not cut out to be a runner.* Forty yards later, I'm under the kavu-blue skies, sun glaring off the wind-swept snowdrift. *This is a glorious afternoon! I will run forever!* Just like that, I'm as changeable as the season.

What happens to us when we can no longer see that big things are small, and small things are big? Is this the fear that overwhelms us in our darkest moments? Do we forget that *this too shall pass?*

I throw a snowball for the brown dog. Ever happy, ever smelling the urine evidence of unmet friends, she chases it into the sunlight, bites the snow and bounces toward me, face white, canine mouth somehow grinning.

I would argue that happiness is made up of the many small experiences in a day that bring us joy or contentment. It is in that first sip of coffee, how my daughter sneaks under the covers with me, when the wind sings in the trees, when hummingbirds pause on a blossom, when friends make me laugh, when my frozen face is suddenly warmed again by the afternoon sun.

I like my Subaru, don't get me wrong. Mostly it is a transportation device of clutter, medical references, markers, mud, and hair. Also, equipment for about seventeen alternative sports (which do make me happy). It's just a thing though. Things can be replaced. I've lost a few in my day. Cars, homes, a red bike I loved that got stolen.

Humans, memories, and experiences, they cannot be replaced. Even by the basic laws of economics, this makes them of unique value. It seems, thus, we ought to value those things, however small, more than the big things: cars, houses, debts, regrets.

I round a corner and watch the awkward, eager paws of Freya slide out on the ice as she crashes down. She leaps up high into the air, as if she, too, finds hilarity in her adolescent clumsiness. It makes me happy to watch her. It reminds me to be playful in my life.

Today is a dark day in a dark time. The overwhelming sadness cannot be ignored, but there is a peaceful acceptance of it out here on my run. The sun is setting in the west, the few clouds are lining with a bright silver.

I am not a superstitious girl, but the afternoon rays of sunlight seem like a gentle reminder from beyond. Somewhere, someone has found peace within and wants us to know we have peace within us too. We must just remember the small things, and that many small things make for a wonderful life.

It is amazing how much joy I can find in the seemingly benign. Such as taking a hot shower in my own house for a change.

I pitter-patter around the last corner toward my car. Now I'm happy for the car too. The whole drive home, I think about how glorious that simple, infinite hot shower will feel on my chilled bones. How happy my warm and dry clothes will make me.

When the seemingly big things come and weigh us down, fill us with fear and impossibility, we must turn to the small ones. We might just find that the love and light there are the constants we need to go on.

The Gentle Reminders of
Mother Nature

I DON'T ALWAYS LIKE GOING OUTSIDE. Outside it is cold and wet. The snow, apparently here to stay this year, is deep and heavy. Some days, going outside is obligatory because I have a running coach who might send me texts in ALL CAPS if I miss a workout. Those days, I can't quite see outside of myself.

Yet transformation is inevitable. Go outside, watch dogs leap and bound with carefree joy, look up to see the distant white mountains. Eventually, the cloud over my brain will dissipate and clarity will come, like enlightenment to a meditator. Or so I assume (otherwise, sitting still just seems like a waste of time).

On this day, though, I can't shake it. My snowshoes are rubbing. The snow is far too deep, and I've worn my flimsy pair. Every step is as hard as the work going on in my head. I rant and rage in my mind. It is an invisible war in there.

I play a game with myself: think of *anything* and see what happens. I choose car tires, and within a moment, I am furious at the entire wheel industry, the chore of changing tires for the season, the time I got a ticket for having my studs on too late, and on and on. I could get mad at crème brûlée, and it's only Wednesday.

I decide if I'm going to suffer anyway, I might as well suffer with intention, and I trudge even harder through the snow. I sink with every step. The dogs keep walking on the back of my shoes and tripping me. My body is hot, but my hands are cold. I only ate a banana for breakfast, and now I'm starving.

My pity party is in full swing when I break through a snow bridge and come crashing down into a creek. I let out a small cry as I flail about trying to catch myself. The dogs, ever loyal, land on top of me to lick my face with concern, and I sink deeper into the snowy, watery chasm.

I can't get out. The more I struggle, the more the snow caves in around me. My shoes are pinned at an impossible angle. Water is rushing around me as I shove dogs and snow off me. I'm not getting anywhere. *#%@! snowshoeing.

I capitulate to Mother Nature and my predicament. I stop moving and listen to the silence. Snow absorbs all the sounds but for the water rushing beneath me. I take a deep breath, then methodically pull snow down to pack it so I can leverage a lift. The series of chaotic lurching and breakdance moves to follow are what I imagined it to look like if the Abominable Snowman had a seizure while wearing a cupcake beanie. Somehow, at the end of it, I am out of the creek and on the safer side of it.

I laugh as I pull the snow out of my pants and shirt. *Okay, Universe, I hear you. Loud and clear.*

Suddenly, I am grateful that I have a car and studded tires. What do I have to complain about? It's Wednesday, and I am out hiking in my backyard with my dogs because I can. I'm healthy and I have free time, and even though I live in eternal winter, all the logistics of capitalism allow me to eat *fair trade organic bananas* for breakfast.

I pick up the pace because I'm soaked and far from home. The only way to stay warm is to keep moving fast. The loop is long, but I'm on the shorter end of it. I've forgotten all the things from earlier as I happily consider the warm fire and hot coffee awaiting me.

Just as I round the final corners toward my house, I see my dogs ahead approaching an enormous moose. He's right in the middle of the narrow road, and working around him means a wide-berth detour in steep, snow-covered cliffs. I'm watching my dogs and considering if I need to command them to bark or heel as they near the bull.

They are wagging their tails, quiet, and *greeting* the moose like he could be our family horse. And the moose doesn't mind. He smells them right back and walks lazily down the road with them. I pitter-patter behind until he steps into some cedars to let us by. I issue a cheerful, "Good Morning, Mr. Moose" as I trot toward my cabin.

"Indeed, it is," he replies in silent moose telepathy speak as he contentedly chews on a branch.

Climbing Kilimanjaro:
The One-Item Bucket List

SOME MONTHS AGO, my friend Shawn was diagnosed with terminal cancer. It's the kind of news that would have me buried in pints of ice cream and trying to get a head start on morphine pills. But not Shawn. Shawn said he had one thing on his bucket list: Climb Kilimanjaro.

We gathered a small group of naive and inexperienced people with, apparently, lots of money and time on their hands, and headed to Tanzania with our North Face duffels (we at least *looked* legit) and sun block. There are a lot of different ways to climb a mountain, but Kilimanjaro almost forces a kind of mountaineering luxury. Guides and porters are mandatory.

"This isn't our *usual* kind of trip," my friend Sarah says. I'm hoping that by this she merely means we won't get lost this time, but she is referring to the extensive staff that are going to facilitate our climb. If I'm ever diagnosed with cancer, please remind me how nice it is to have someone else pack my tent while I start my ascent each morning.

Regardless of the village of locals helping our crew up the mountain, we had to at least dress ourselves and schlepp one slow foot in front of the other as we trekked first through the jungle, then the high heather, and then into the moonscape slopes above 16,000 ft.

Mother Nature must have heard our elitist, self-reliant complaints and decided to complicate our 'hike up' route with a few feet of uncommon snow. Most of the porters had never seen snow. My guide, making his 203rd summit, told me that it has been more than 15 years since they had snowfall like this. We did not tell the rest of our party but instead acted like this was all standard trekking experience.

"Shouldn't we have crampons and ice axes for these steep, snow-covered slopes?"

"No," I say. "Just don't fall because you won't stop."

I casually ask Sarah if this qualifies as an alpine climb, and she scoffs at my drama and says, "No. This is a snow-covered trail."

I pass the word along because people don't really plummet to their deaths on snow-covered trails, so we're probably safe. As long as no one actually does plummet to their death.

As we grind our way upward on our summit attempt, the weather changes by the minute, and the conversation dwindles to occasional health checks. I look down the white expanse blotched with exposed volcanic rock and watch this unlikely crew of climbers pick their way up one of the Seven Summits. They don't even know how awesome they are. Or how sunburned.

It is a reminder to me: Anyone can do any damn thing they want. You don't have to be some experienced mountaineer to go after it. You don't have to have the fancy gear, the record, the ripped abs, or the right genes. You just need a bunch of crazy friends who are willing to support your ideas, share their energy bars, and not judge you when you start vomiting at 18,200 ft. They are allowed to make fun of you later at camp, though.

I've climbed a lot of mountains in my day, and I'm pretty sure I will climb more, but none will move me as this one has. Don't let anyone tell you it's an easy hike up, either – no one hikes easily at 19,341 ft. Cresting that final ridge after making the Western Breach, seeing the summit sign in the snowy distance, the choked back tears came in full force.

There is something about a summit that fills the soul with profound gratitude. I don't know if this was Shawn's intention for reaching the Roof of Africa, but as we stood there on the top of Uhuru Peak, each of us expressed the same message of thankfulness.

We can overcome mountains, even while cancer is overcoming us. Sometimes that mountain is just getting out of bed in the morning. Sometimes it's Kilimanjaro. And every day of our blessed lives, we can share in the experiences and friendships that make those mountains a little less intimidating and life a little more meaningful. Climb on, my friends, whatever your mountain is.

Mother Nature Has Its Own Plans for My Garden

THIS SPRING, my garden is going to be done *right*. I spent the winter getting educated on books like *Tomatoes Love Carrots* and encyclopedias of homesteading. I know that wooden pallets work great for building compost bins, that birch burns wet, that aphid problems can be solved with ladybugs.

I special-ordered ladybugs and praying mantises on the internet and hatched them on my counter. I drew maps of my garden and color-coded the rows according to how much sun they get. I labeled it carefully with all the advice of the best companion planting manuals. I even *got my soil tested.*

The report came back: "Looks like you live on a granite hilltop with clay." Then there was some stuff about copper and calcium, and all I heard in my head was lalala. I went to the gardening store.

"I need some stuff for my soil. Some kind of meals? Blood? Bone?" I never knew, aside from a pathological desire to kill ground squirrels, that gardening was such a macabre hobby.

They had all the meals. I said I needed five pounds of each meal. The girl looked at me like I was a mad permaculture wildcrafter or something and slowly poured the equivalent of blood crystals into my brown bag. I grinned. No rabbit is going to chew through a veritable carcass mush to get to my chard this year.

I also made use of my greenhouse. I recognize the amount of preparedness, organization, and time is impressive. Not everyone is this dedicated or well-prepared. This is going to be a hallelujah garden if I ever saw one. For weeks, the solarium attached to my home has been a bed of seed starts. If my sprout-eating dog even *looks* at them, I wave my arms in a hysteric wail until she opts to smell the ants that have moved into the room.

Now I know about ants though. I have anti-ant arsenals. First, I used corn starch. *Eat that, suckers!* I thought. Four minutes later, the corn starch pile was gone. My ant problem might have been worse than I thought. I put more out. I looked up how to do that borax and sugar mixture. The ants kept cleaning up the corn starch. *Fine,* I thought, *eat all the starch you want, silly ants.*

It took me a few days to realize the white spot on my brown dog's nose was corn starch. Like some worn-out coke addict, I busted her one morning in the flower beds, a pile of slobber where the starch had been.

I switched to borax in the garden and painted my fruit trees with that sticky feet stuff. I found an ant nest and obliterated it, then had nightmares about them raiding my house.

A single asparagus popped out of the soil last week. Asparagus! Robust and healthy, I planned for days what kind of steak I would eat with it. I would make a meal of mostly Hollandaise sauce and this single stalk. It would be glorious.

I went out later in the week to transplant some seedlings. The asparagus had been eaten. I checked the varmint trap. It had been pushed away from the hole to their den. Apparently, it was blocking their main entrance, and they needed to get a large stalk of asparagus in there for a guest party.

The day I went out to plant all the seed starts, a storm came and hailed onto me and my efforts as I made a mad dash to get the delicate little babies in the ground, risking instant death by lightning. I would sacrifice myself for prize cabbage. Two days later, those that survived were scorched by the sun.

I stopped keeping score, but I'm pretty sure Mother Nature is winning. One evening, I poured myself a glass of red wine, possibly a rather tall glass, and sipped it intentionally as I meandered down to the garden. I needed to be emotionally stunted before witnessing the carnage. I'll be buying my vegetables at the over-priced organic market this year, no doubt, but at least I'll have already spent a small fortune on killing my own.

In the garden, a single stalk of new asparagus was poking up. The optimist in me started planning Friday night's meal all over again as a ladybug landed on my hand.

Midlife Crisis for Backwoods Girls

I DON'T NEED A FAST CAR. Fast cars are low to the ground and red and wouldn't make it past the first gravel pitch of my driveway on a good day. These are the things I contemplated on the week of my official entry to middle-age.

Forty is the new twenty, I told myself, but then why the urge to panic about where I am, or where I am not, in life?

Here I am, the proud owner of ten acres of granite hilltop with a variety of trees that I cannot identify and a timber-framed house that I don't know how to repair. How did this even happen?

The panic grew until I manically decided I must learn all the skills to survive the apocalypse, which as far as I can tell, is about the same amount of drama as turning forty.

I called my sparky – the kilt-wearing Mormon – and asked him to come explain the entire science of solar energy from Sun to *what kind of batteries do I actually own?*

"You don't know?"

"Right, but I rarely admit that. I say things like 'they have about twice the storage capacity and amp hours of my old system' because then I sound like I know what I'm talking about."

He scribbled some basic calculations for me: 12 X 2 = 24.

My novice level of basic skills and rudimentary math (try calculating amp hours and solar input, then figuring out how long you can run a curling iron) only worsened my fears. I was going to die alone and buried in the snow because I burned the wrong wood or something. Or made a hydrogen bomb in my pantry.

I scoured my Homesteader's Manual. It wouldn't stick, probably because my brain is atrophying at an exponential rate since my birthday. It was on a Monday. By Tuesday, my ovaries had shriveled into raisins, my hair was turning gray, and my mailbox was filling with sweepstakes post.

I thought that midlife crisis meant I'd buy a fast car and develop a bunch of swank new hobbies, like paragliding and road cycling. Instead, I wanted to learn how to fell trees and equalize batteries.

How I've made it this far in life without knowing how to run a chainsaw baffles me. That might fly in the big city, but I live in Idaho. Seems like chainsaw slingin' should at least be a class in junior high or something. I probably took sex education instead, my priorities always a little askew.

So, I called a friend who is a veritable force of a logger and asked him to show me how to run a chainsaw in a manner that would preserve my limbs while also supplying my firewood for the season. He showed up on a Sunday morning, forced me to wear an entire suit of bright orange, and dropped a tree exactly where he said he would.

"Now you try," he said.

"Are all saws this heavy?"

He said most were heavier.

I plopped my earmuffs on, dropped my faceguard, and fired up that chainsaw. I cut the tree this way, then that way, and then it fell right where I wanted it to as well. I limbed it and cut it into firewood. I may have done some sort of strange lumberjack dance afterward.

The apocalypse can come.

I remembered the studies I've read on how learning new things helps maintain the integrity of our brains as we age. I assume it also keeps us from getting bored when we retire. That is, if I haven't overzealously clearcut my entire property by then. Running a chainsaw was more fun than I thought. Come to think of it, so is aging.

Tenant Troubles for
Backwoods Landlords

I AM NOT SURE IF THERE IS EVER a particularly pleasant place in which to encounter a nest of wasps, but I am sure that doing so while dangling from a rope, twenty feet off the ground, is *not* one of them. Also, if this homesteading-off-the-grid life doesn't quite work out for me, I'm pretty sure I am qualified to join a circus.

The day had started out like any good day: with coffee, blue skies, and a chore list. My sparky was scheduled to arrive in the cool morning hours and explain the science of solar power to me while we adjusted the panels. While curious about exactly *how* the sun makes my washing machine work, I was more curious about whether he'd wear his standard issue kilt on a rooftop job.

He arrived in disappointingly practical shorts, and we set to the task of mounting a series of ladders onto my steep metal roof.

"This ladder is not fixed to anything!" I yelled up at him, wearing my full climbing harness and looking as though I were about to summit some impressive alpine peak. "Are you sure OSHA would approve?"

The sound that extension ladders make when you climb them is ominous. There is a hollow could-break-any-minute-because-you-eat-too-much-pie sort of chink and rattle as one ascends. It does not offer any measure of confidence to the climber.

I had two birds to kill with one stone this morning. My solar panels needed to be adjusted to a better angle for the season, and I needed to plug the hole the woodpecker drilled in my siding last summer.

I shot that woodpecker with a BB gun. I didn't want to kill him; I just wanted him to suffer a similar agony to the brain-shattering, dream-jolting, 4 a.m.-wake-up-jackhammer sound I was experiencing every morning. The hole he was drilling was approximately three feet away from my bed. I hated to hurt him, but not as much as I hated that alarm. I was chuffed when he moved to the woodpile with the beetles instead.

Until the squirrels found his hole.

They made a wall-condo and raised a family there. I could hear them playing Monopoly and arguing about dinner, but mostly it was the morning rush that bothered me. And so I banged on the wall with a King James (unsure of where this literature came from, but pleased with its banging efficacy) until they moved out. It was only a matter of time until some other family of tree rodents moved in.

On this morning, determined for a permanent solution to my tenant problem, I drilled an anchor into the wall. I clung to my rickety ladder system, then clipped in with a short line. I needed just enough length to safely dangle around the corner with a board to cover the hole. I had a tool belt (pink, thanks Dad!) stuffed with nails and a heavy hammer swinging from my hip.

I looked down. *Don't look down!* I'm not afraid of heights; I am merely afraid of plummeting to my death next to a gas can and a generator. It's just not very romantic.

I swung off the edge of the roof and lodged the end of my hammer under the damaged board, then gave it a good yank and plucked it off the wall. There was a strange noise following.

Suddenly, a dozen, angry, fat yellowjackets ejected from the exposed framing. I believe all yellowjackets are angry, but these ones seemed *particularly* irate. Probably because they had just taken over the lease from the squirrels.

Wasps make an angry sound, and it is not something you want to hear when you are tethered helplessly to a roof with only about three feet of play. The angry wasps and their friends started rushing out of the hole looking for the culprit. I pointed at the electrician.

I wonder if they are like dinosaurs and they can't see me if I don't move? To move also meant doing some sort of interpretive dance to swing my way back onto the roof, unclipping, and teetering down that blasted ladder. Would I rather be: a) secure but pelted by an angry mob or b) unsecured while trying to outrun said angry mob?

I opted for the former, shoved a couple of framing nails in my mouth, swung toward the exposed hole, and slammed my board decidedly over it.

I missed by an inch, which resulted in a string of swearwords only understood by troubled homeowners. You know who you are. The next swing was on target, and I drove that first nail in with a shaky, determined swing, then followed with no less than 42 more nails, possibly impaling most of the wasps in the process. Trembling and out of nails, I stopped to catch my breath and fight off any stray insects.

"Hey, careful over there," yelled Sparky from a safe distance. "There might be a yellowjacket nest."

Mountain Medicine for the Soul

THEY SAY THAT WE CANNOT RUSH OUR HEALING, but I am pretty sure "they" just don't hike enough.

The mountains, along with the immeasurable joy and suffering they can bring, are a potent tincture of healing that I return to often. This time, with the specific intention of slathering the balm of their glacial views and alpine lake water on the wounds of a broken heart. As always, they provide me a new sense of perspective – usually a blatant reminder that my sorrows are as impermanent and unimportant as the latest shoe fashion.

Mountains are also a reminder that all things have a life cycle, even relationships. Thus far, I have not been effective at manifesting one with a lifespan any longer than the success of home shopping network kitchen gadgets. French fry dicers and vacuum hair trimmers have more marketable longevity than dating me. I have a set of kitchen knives that have diced their way through the entire soap opera dynasty of my adult life.

It is not for lack of trying on anyone's part, but rather a blatant kind of optimism that is swaddled in the ability to see the elevated potential in anything and anyone. I'm pretty sure it is this exact same optimism that gets me into trouble in the mountains.

A park ranger is showing me a trail that winds up a canyon to Ball Pass in the Canadian Rockies. This time, I'm so jaded, I need to go nurse my injuries in a foreign country. He's talking in kilometers, and I basically half everything he says in my head as he shows me the turnaround point ten kilometers in.

"What are all these little lake things over here? Is that a *trail* to those little lake things?!" I ask.

He checks the system and tells me the trail is clear with patches of snow on the passes, there have been no bear sightings, and it's about fifty kilometers if I cut corners.

The optimism is strong on this day. I cut myself some trail snacks with a Ginsu knife I bought myself for Christmas in college, still capable of slicing aluminum cans with the same efficacy that I sever myself from boyfriend candidates. Then I hike from BC to Alberta.

It's a long climb that starts with a deceptively delightful meandering through fields of spring flowers, winds its way along a creek, provides all the enticing rewards of the journey without any of the mosquitoes or ceaseless scree slogs to come. "This is great!" I am thinking as I trot up the trail happily for miles. And miles. And nearly twice as many kilometers.

The analogy is perfect. The first pass is bliss, and I'm not even tired. *Look at the incredible glacial views! It was so worth the work!* Four hours later, I'm dancing at a creekside, swatting mosquitoes while I filter water desperately, wondering what the bloody purpose of these bugs is anyway as they threaten to carry me away like the flying monkeys in *The Wizard of Oz*.

Four hours after that, I'm standing on the edge of another alpine lake, watching the sun set behind granite peaks. There is no wind. The water makes no sound. A kind of peace exists there, a stillness and contentment that appears to only be achieved when all other options have been exhausted.

In many ways, the mountains are my lover. I return to them again and again, to confide in them, to be consoled by them, and to scale the summits of ecstasy that must be experienced rather than imagined.

Four hours after that, I am still crossing creeks and crawling under logs in the night air. I don't mind the tired legs, the chill, the fact that I had two energy bars for dinner, the scratches and bites, the fear of bears. It is not stamina that I lack, but perhaps that expectations are excessive.

It was after midnight when I reached the car. Worn out yet filled up, the tiny fibers of my heart were mending as those of my legs were aching. The mountains had provided once more, and somehow, they always seem to exceed my expectations.

That Time a Worst Nightmare Came True

WHEN YOU LIVE ALONE IN THE MOUNTAINS with a kid, relying on solar power and YouTube instructional videos to keep your house running, you have a different set of fears than the general population. Among mine: a string of cloudy days, carburetor issues on my chainsaw, and head lice.

The latter has been a concern of mine since my chiclet attended the hippie socialist kindergarten in the forests of Germany, where lice and ticks were a daily warning. While we plucked many a tick off her tiny body, we somehow managed to escape the infestation of other critters.

So as one might imagine, the flood of vitriol that emitted from my vocal cords subsequent to that fatal phone call was hardly appropriate for printed publication.

"Uhm, the kids have lice."

These phone calls always happen at approximately 10 o'clock in the evening when said single mother is running around like a banshee trying to pack the last items for a desert camping trip departing at sunrise. That is always a super convenient time to locate some head chemo and start shampooing, well, *everything*.

Lice, as far as I am concerned, are the minor's version of an STD. They even come with all the social stigma and snake oil cures, though I couldn't find anyone treating lice with mercury. This was somewhat of a relief because I'd read Casanova's autobiography, and by the time he died, he'd consumed enough mercury to land himself on the far end of the crazy spectrum.

(Whereas prior to that, he was just in the middle but without a moral compass.)

I immediately set the phone down, finished my swear rant that was beginning to sound like Brooklyn slam poetry, and started combing through my daughter's fine, blonde hair. I felt like a primate, except I wasn't compelled to eat anything. Much to my dismay, I found lice.

This discovery was followed with a robust heebie-jeebies dance across the bathroom floor where I hoped that the sheer force of my emotional repulsion would eject the critters. This was not the case. In fact, they seemed perfectly content to wiggle their way along strands of hair, ignoring my hysteria and doing whatever such parasites do. It was a Thursday, probably trivia night or something at the local dive behind the right ear.

Not quite sure what one actually does to eradicate such a visitor, and unable to convince my eleven-year-old to shave her head, I briefly considered finding some Napalm on the dark web. I couldn't locate any studies confirming the efficacy of this treatment for anything less nefarious than war crimes, so I sourced a box of some ominous looking shampoo at the pharmacy. They keep it right next to all the other embarrassing purchases like hemorrhoid cream, prophylactics, and reading glasses.

The directions said, "Leave on for ten minutes," but I left it on until my scalp felt like a gastric ulcer and my child complained of burning eyes. If anything, our hair would just fall out and the problem would resolve itself. After we'd washed our hair and I'd stopped dry heaving, we did no less than fourteen hundred loads of laundry before sunrise. The last thing you want in the desert is a colony of lice on your scalp, in your tent, far from running water.

The second degree burns on my skin must have been at least moderately effective, and it would appear that the post-shampoo itching was mostly related to the chemical exposure. *Surely* no lice would survive that!

Ten days later, like life cycle clockwork, the little buggers reappeared, just a few stragglers, genetic anomalies. This time, we were prepared with all the hippie sauce one could imagine, and the world's tiniest comb. Our new nightly ritual is extensive haircare, washing linens, and drinking snake oil. Though if I find any more little bugs, I'm going to ignore my own moral compass and invite Monsanto to make me some shampoo.

At least these sunny days are keeping the batteries charged for my 24-hour laundering operation. And sleeping in fresh sheets every night isn't half bad either.

Knitting Season Arrives with Misguided Optimism

EVERY SEASON THAT COMES, I sigh with relief at the end of the associated seasonal labor and optimistically plan what I will do with all my free time.

Now that my firewood is in, the defunct garden has been ignored into submission, and I've shop-vacuumed most of the live wasps into dust bag death, I believe knitting season has officially begun.

Knitting season is a glorious time of the year. During knitting season, evenings are spent huddled around a small fortune of natural fibers while listening to some novel with my kid. We make Christmas gifts and peruse sweater catalogs and usually there is a pot of butternut squash on the stove, permeating the house with promise of autumnal delight.

The problem with knitting season is that it lands on a Tuesday most years, and I probably have a damn PTA meeting that night. By the time I get the stove pipe cleaned, the hoses drained, the bark raked, the burn piles ready, and the broken lawn mower appropriately covered for winter (I let it air out all summer just in case sunshine heals carburetors), the snow starts falling.

This marks the beginning of snow management season which involves far less sleigh riding than I expected.

I seem to recall several books by Laura Ingalls Wilder in which the entire family got to sit around after sundown and knit or sew each other wedding dresses by hand. This had no small part in my decision to live in a cabin in the woods. Maybe a house on the prairie is key there and I missed the obvious.

Once the snow starts falling, there is shoveling and gear drying and, my personal favorite, layering up like a Siberian in a storm to go plow my sketchy hillside driveway. There is also ice removal on the deck, ice removal on the stairs, fires that need to be made, lit, stoked. Wood that must be hauled. The soot, bark, and mud clean up that follows the migration of Tamarack logs from one pile to another pile.

This is precisely why I have been working on the same exact sweater for about four years now. It's for my mom. Every birthday and Christmas, I present her with the latest addition. "For Christmas this year, I made you the armpit!" Occasionally, we have a wet fall and I can get through a beanie or half a sock before I'm outside moving my roof avalanche.

Snow removal season typically threatens to never end. Just when I think it will and I start looking at new sweaters to start-but-not-finish, there's a late March dump that reminds me nature is called 'Mother' because she's fickle (a decidedly sexist observation).

As those last feet of snow start giving way to soil, I am so grateful for the end of the season because it is surely more work than any other season. Now at last, I might have time to get another armpit knit.

Then the seed catalogs start showing up. This marks the beginning of gardening season, a veritable plant crime at my house. There is lots of fanfare about spraying seedlings in the greenhouse and running irrigation hoses and devising death traps for rodents. I could save everyone including the rodents a lot of hardship by just going to the Farmer's Market instead. But no, I have a vision of summer mornings with my coffee, weeding happily with the butterflies, and harvesting our efforts. The latter rarely occurs, but the fantasy remains.

It really isn't until the end of summer that I realize all my best intentions for enjoying the season of less chores have been missed. Mostly because I have camping gear to clean, coolers to scrub, paddleboards to store, bikes to tune.

Yet every year I have the same expectation: "This summer is going to be so *relaxing*. I will not overcommit myself." And every year, as fall creeps upon us with its glorious cool mornings and soft afternoon warmth, I sigh with optimism and short-term memory loss and think, "Thank goodness this busy summer is over. I can finally sit down and get some knitting done."

Every Good Parent Takes Family to Burning Man for Vacation

IT WASN'T THAT I'D ALWAYS DREAMED of going to Burning Man. I had taken my daughter on another epic outdoor adventure, complete with snowfield traverses, sketchy river crossings, and unexpected miles of just-a-little-farther. It was no surprise when she wrapped up that trip by asking, "Can't we just go look at some art like normal families?"

We're not really a normal family, but I knew just the place where such people actually look at art. So I got online and found us some tickets to the legendary desert art cultural movement known as Burning Man. Because all good parents take their kids to a naked party of radical expressionism, electronica, and mind-expanding substances.

Having never actually been to Burning Man, I guessed there was much research to be done. First and foremost, we found a special camp within the temporary city of Black Rock where children and families are especially welcome. They have snow cones and a rule that excludes midday orgies, which I assumed were everywhere else.

"Oh my," said the vitamin lady at the health food store. "You know there are *naked people* there." She was very concerned, but I proudly noted that my European child had, more than once, witnessed several grown German men playing volleyball in the nude because they could. She was far less emotionally scarred than I was. How they haven't made it an Olympic sport yet, I do not know.

We raided all the thrift stores, declared our camp Queens of the Night Sky, packed our bags and headed for the Nevada desert. We had read the guides and understood the basics: Bring sunscreen, leave absolutely no trace (that means your gray water too), don't forget the goggles, and we said *leave no trace.* We felt as prepared as rookies could be. Logistically, we were. Emotionally, we had no idea.

In the middle of the desert, seventy-some-odd humans in campers, cars, planes, and parachutes descend upon the playa in a cloud of white dust, thumping bass, and a sense of community I have never elsewhere witnessed. From a barren landscape, up rises an entire city of organized streets, impressive order, and a port-a-potty logistical miracle.

There are the things one hears of: stop and go traffic upon entry, whiteout dust storms, nudity, pasties, men in tutus, art, music, psychedelics, but nothing ever that I have read or seen comes close to portraying the visceral experience of *being there.*

The only thing more awe-inspiring than standing in the middle of the bustling, thumping, whirring, laughing scene was watching my eleven-year-old daughter take it all in. It was a sense of wonder, excitement, curiosity, compassion, and social responsibility I have seldom seen in the same year, not to mention the same hour. And every hour of every day was just this kind of delightful excursion.

"Do you have a reservation?" asks the maître d'.

I am standing in my flip-flops, feet white from the playa dust, holding a cup of coffee. The sun has just come up, and the row of port-a-potties before me has no line. I blink. The man is wearing a tuxedo and a top hat. He has a white towel over one arm, a neat folder in the other.

"No?" he says. "Well, let me see what I can do for you."

Just as he finishes speaking, we hear the clap-clank of a door slamming, and a sleepy-eyed camper wanders off.

"Oh look! Something just opened up!" he cheers as he shuffles me toward the john.

I registered for the Burning Man 50k, showing up before five in the morning to a crowd of happy runners, just like at any race except a brave few were naked. (My favorite being the guy wearing only a watch, shoes, and a pulse band around his chest.) Thousands of acres of candy-colored art exhibitions lit up the horizon.

It was pancake flat, four loops around what is known as 'the deep playa' – or the part of Black Rock City that is dedicated to the art. The famed art cars came out to set up temporary aid stations while the spectators sang, danced, and offered margaritas. I ran most of the race next to a man in his sixties wearing a pink bikini. He was an English teacher, a grandfather, a veteran, and had run more miles in his life than I could dream up. This, he said, is one of his favorite events. The art keeps the mind busy.

There is no commerce at Burning Man, so the sense of generosity and the way our culture has somehow unlearned the art of receiving was palpable. My daughter and I, wearing frocks and goggles, riding our bikes through the streets with grins and a conversation that was constantly stimulated by what we witnessed, were overwhelmed with the offers. Snow cones and unlawful waffles and bluegrass concerts and yoga classes and church services for name-your-denomination.

She went to every activity she could cram into her day: robot building, recycling how-tos, tutu tutorials, blind fruit tasting, art car tours, the giant hammock, the roller-skating rink, the farmer's market. And then she made a dozen new friends: children from all walks of life, from all geographical locations, thrown together in the same village of little people.

In the mornings, I would walk through the quiet camp (possibly the only quiet place at Burning Man) and see piles of gypsy children sleeping on trampolines in a mess of blankets, tangled limbs, stuffed animals, dusty faces, and dreams.

I watched each day as my own daughter's horizons expanded into a world where anything is possible, all ideas are accepted, and kindness is a given. It was a world where the individuals mattered, the community mattered, the planet *mattered*. But not much else did.

What did not matter to her: what someone's job was, whether they had clothes on or not, their religion, or if they drove a Tesla.

"It's hot today," she said, grabbing a spray bottle of water and her hat. "The girls and I are going to stand on the corner and spray people who want it to help keep everyone cool."

I took my granny's ashes to the temple along with the memories of a decade-long marriage that bruised both body and heart. I left my notes there on the wood to rise into the cosmos with the flames, hopeful they would dissipate like my pain. The wooden temple was the temporal vessel of a thousand hurts and losses, a place that pulls the tears from your eyes, reminds us that suffering and joy are not that different from each other, and that each of us knows them both.

We've taken a lot of vacations around the world, but nothing opened our hearts or awakened our souls in the same way. Burning Man works hard to avoid a label, and perhaps that is just right. It is what each of us takes away from it. For my daughter and me, it was a gentle reminder of the beauty of humanity, of how profound and important our connection to each other is, and that, without exception, all are welcome.

Rehabilitation for the Resistant

"DON'T YOU DARE TELL ME TO TAKE UP SWIMMING," I warn the surgeon who is visibly struggling not to roll his eyes.

Along with knitting, chopping wood, and eating, my other hobby is being the worst nightmare of medical experts. I particularly love pre-diagnosing myself and strutting in with a list of things I will and won't do, then demanding they prescribe a therapy that involves lots of running, cookie consumption, and is guaranteed to reduce my pain. Preferably immediately.

After the kind (and impressively patient) doctor explains the technology of an MRI while his scribe tries to figure out how to accurately chart my swear words, the abbreviated diagnosis is revealed: I've torn about 70% of my hamstring away from the bone.

I respond as I usually do. "Does this mean I should run less? Why don't you have cookies in the waiting room? Do you even *have* a medical degree?"

I had actually been trying running therapy for the past five months or so. Not surprisingly, it wasn't improving. I was waking up at night in pain and I couldn't figure out what kind of injury would get worse from sleeping. Bodies are sort of baffling things. Unless you're a hip version of a surgeon in loafers, apparently.

I choke back tears on an exam table, cuddling my dog while receiving an injection that requires direct access to all the glory of my backside. Medical procedures that reveal my fear of induced pain while having my skivvies around my knees tend to be my least favorite kind, somewhere right up there with dental work or having a member of the mafia remove my toenails (I imagine).

Even as I am hobbling out of the office, I am concocting a plan to use and abuse my body heavily until physical therapy starts the next week. If no one with a medical degree has specifically told me not to do the things, then I'm going to do the things *hard* while I still can.

"Next week," I promise myself, "I'll slow down." Because it is autumn and the trees are glorious in their flaming colors, leaves raining down in orange and red on the paths. I want to kick leaves and smell the chilling earth and see the contrasting blue skies. Besides, if I finish tearing this hammy off the bone, they'll fix me right up. Either way, it looks like I'll finally finish a knitting project or two this winter.

My plan is to go to Whitefish and mountain bike with friends. The Tamarack forests are florescent, bright with iridescent colors that light up the sky. When the sun goes down, everything still glows yellow-green. The needles will fall soon and leave bright orange piles on the soil, or if the snow falls, decorate the white carpet with a kind of golden jewelry.

The trails, the laughter of friends, the beating of my heart all erase the memory of the week. I'm gentle on my body and I thank it for gifting me with these experiences. I pledge some self-care and rest, make some amends and apologies, and promise things will be different in the future. I sound like the abusive spouse of my limbs and joints.

The cosmos, it would appear, does not believe me either. I crash my bike. From a stationary position. *How does this happen,* one might ask. Some accidents take particular talent to achieve. And in this slow-motion debacle of a woman, clipped into her pedals, arm flailing behind her, unable to stop the fated impact, gravity and other laws of physics win the battle. I come crashing down, and body parts move into places they should not.

Curled up on my knees, I am heaving, trying not to vomit or cry at the same time because this situation could only be more tragic and comical if I choke on my regurgitated energy bar. It takes me a few moments to recover, and when I stand up, my riding buddy is giving me a nod.

"You, uh, want me to reduce that shoulder for you?" he asks.

My arm is dangling awkwardly. My fingers are already numb. This is when you're grateful that your friends are chiropractors. He tromps a few dried-up ferns, kicks a rock out of the way, and gestures to his impromptu office. Then he does a textbook reduction of a dislocated shoulder. I like it slightly more than the rear-end injection, probably because I get to keep my pants on.

We get back on our bikes and ride home in the waning evening light. The tamaracks illuminate our way. With a bum right leg and a wonky left shoulder, at least I won't be swimming in circles.

A Guide to Developing Intimacy
in the Outdoors

IT IS NO SECRET THAT SOME OUTDOORS PEOPLE might struggle with intimacy when it comes to other humans and thus spend much time in the wilderness where humans are few and far between. When they do happen across another, they most certainly will have at least one thing in common.

Some time ago, I was running in the state forest land behind my home in the Selkirks when I ran into another human. I see a lot of moose and the occasional elk. I never see other humans. For this reason, I can run wearing what one might expect to see in a 1986 Jazzercise video, including leg warmers and mascara melting down my face. I might have to chop my own wood, but I can do it in my underwear if I please – just one of the many benefits of backwoods living.

I figured this gentleman and his wife were lost, and they figured I'd fallen off a bus returning from a Las Vegas bachelorette party. It turned out that they lived a few hills away and had done so for nearly three decades. In fact, they had been hiking and mapping the "trails" for years.

I asked how to get to the top of a particular mountain that I had attempted from various angles without success. "There *must* be a trail to the top," I said.

He drew back a little and eyeballed me from head to toe in an obvious assessment of my personal character. I wished I had at least worn matching socks.

"If I show you on the map, you have to promise to never tell anyone with a machine," he said.

Fair enough.

Several weeks later, I came home to find a hand-drawn map on my kitchen counter with miles of unmarked trails. Some of them I had discovered on my own lost-most-of-the-day adventures; others were unknown treasures of cedar groves and huckleberry patches.

For two years now, I have run these trails. Sometimes, I snowshoe them. Sometimes, I pick the wrong one and end up in someone's backyard. I have come to know every inch, where the best mossy rocks are, where the moose sheds cannot be found (I still don't know where they *can* be found), where the cedar boughs hang low, where it feels like Narnia in the wintertime. I have a thousand little memories of leaping over creeks, stomping in puddles, or realizing how far from home I was without food.

What I don't have is memories of being with anyone else in my own private Idaho. There are lots of memories of a brown dog and a single summit I drag my lady friends up once or twice a year. The rest of it is like my sanctuary.

So, it occurred to me last weekend as I kicked up the snow, turned and chirped to my running partner, "Isn't this little section of trail glorious!?" that I might be in love.

Lord knows, I wouldn't share this with *just anyone*. In fact, I hadn't shared it with anyone. Ever.

There is a purity to a place with only first-person memories. It cannot be tainted with broken hearts or bitterness, even if that is what inspired the journey in the first place. And yet maybe the most vulnerable gesture we can make is to share an invariably unique experience with another human. Maybe letting them into our soul-searching places, our healing woods, the soils that ground us, is like showing the delicate interior of our beating hearts.

While the general population might develop intimacy over candlelit dinners and conversation, the outdoors person likely has a different approach. Evidence of our desire for deep emotional connection may be measured by the uncharted secrets we show, by bringing memories of someone onto our backyard trails, and possibly by how many M&Ms we leave in the trail mix before we offer to share it.

Some Things Are Best Left to the Professionals

I HAVE THIS NEIGHBOR KID who got himself a little plow. He's one of seven children named after confederate generals, which is exactly how I do so well at Trivial Pursuit in the category of "Monuments Removed."

He called me when the snow started falling. "You need someone to plow?"

It takes me about four hours to plow with my own little ATV, but I'm determined to be able to do everything it takes to live independently in the mountains, even at the risk of being labeled a feminist. It's less of a rebellion and more of a stubborn determination.

A legitimate Plow Man with a Real Truck charges a pretty penny to plow out here. Basically, it means that I'll be breaking into my retirement if it snows more than once a month in the winter. Or selling a kidney, but I'm trying to save those to pay for my kid's college.

There are not too many jobs that I don't like when it comes to maintaining my mountain home. I'm not a big fan of cleaning the chimney (although I am happy to report that I installed a much safer rigging system for roof access this year). I'm not excited about pulling tansy, an eternal task. And I pretty much abhor plowing.

It's partly because I'm not just a frigid person, but the kind that sets the stereotype for cold feet in bed. I get bizarrely dysfunctional when I get cold. Like a drunk person who lost it all in the slot machines, I start doing useless, redundant things and muttering nonsense.

Case in point, last week I was headed to the bathroom with a newspaper, a cup of coffee, and a towel when my phone rang.

"I'm jackknifed on the road below your driveway."

The woman who lives in the miniature off-grid cabin on my property apparently hasn't learned to drive like a rally racer just yet. This is an imperative skill to have out here. The final approach to our hilltop home is a sketchy, narrow road that is lined with granite on one side and promises a fantastic rumble-tumble roll or two on the other side.

Some families pray before dinner. We pray before the hill.

I threw on a few layers of wool, down pants, down jacket, fuzzy boots, hats, gloves, and anything else one would wear for the Iditarod, and tromped out to assess the situation.

There is "stuck" and then there is "how-did-this-even-happen stuck." It's the kind where the laws of physics don't apply, and one is left wondering how a Tundra finds itself perched on its bumper on a snowbank, rear tires dangling in the air. It's the kind of stuck that has me digging deep into my bag of Idaho road tricks and coming up empty-handed.

"I can have my friend come help us, though I know you don't like getting help from men," says my neighbor.

This is not true at all. I love getting help from men (or any gender identity), especially when it means I can stay home by the fire while *they* figure out how to unstuck the truck. My calls for help are limited to whether or not that person has the tools to actually improve the situation.

Three hours later, I am lying on the ice under the vehicle, trying to pull chains off with hands that have turned into stumps. My fingers stopped hurting some time ago; now they are just dead, white going blue. And I am not making sense anymore. Let's add "getting unstuck" to that list of chores I'm not fond of.

The snow had started falling hard, and the prospect of plowing had the drunk slot-player ranting in my head. I called my neighbor kid. He came whizzing up the road with some kind of turbo racecar plow toy. I have no idea what it is, but I am pretty sure I need to own one. I watched him from the warmth of my cabin, thawing my frostbit fingers, as he sped back and forth on my driveway, waiting for him to eject himself from slamming into snowbanks so hard.

In fifteen minutes, my driveway was clear. I still had half a cup of hot coffee in my hand. This is how I turned plowing from my least favorite chore into my most favorite chore – having someone else do it. Best forty bucks I ever spent.

When Napping Is Better than Hiking, or Not

I RATHER ASSUMED THAT BEING FICKLE was just part of my female constitution. My motivation and intention to do things one moment might be entirely erased by the immediate desire to take a nap, shove a burrito in my face, or immerse myself in a book. This is why I write most of my appointments in pencil, not to mention my retirement plans.

I woke up one morning this weekend, checked my color-coded planner, and excitedly noted I had drawn a large pink bubble indicating that a snowshoe adventure was planned. This was delayed by some other key tasks: grocery shopping, dropping kid off somewhere, a lazy cup of brew at the coffeehouse. By the time I got back home to my snowshoes, it was gray, soggy, cold, and I wanted a sandwich and a siesta.

I made a passionate argument to my bearded companion. It was logical and persuasive and clearly laid out. The superior, reasonable action of the day would be inaction. There were some great bits in there about "knowing when your body needs rest," about having the quiet house to ourselves, about not having enough daylight left, about all the legitimate work I would be missing if I went out. Also, I really needed to practice the banjo.

Nearly five hours later, on a moonless night, the fog settling over the heavy snow, I was still trudging through the trees and confused about how I had even gotten there.

I think it started with lunch. Celebrating my debate victory, I had happily set to making a conciliatory meal of particular deliciousness. Unaware of the impact that a solid meal would have on me, I was jerked out of my lethargy and a wisp of former adventure intent blew past my nostrils. Or maybe it was mayonnaise.

"We should at least go get some fresh air," someone said. It was probably me.

This is a silly thing to say. In the history of my entire life, I have approximately zero recollection of anything ever ending with just a little fresh air. I probably started a few outings that way, but I doubt I have ever finished one with the same sentiment.

The problem seems to be the top of things. I might be okay with the idea of a mild snowshoe through the Narnian trees until I break through and get a view. Inevitably, the top of something is "nearby." Also, my lack of depth perception proves to be a real problem here. Everything looks attainable, even peaks that are potentially north of the Canadian border.

"I packed a Lärabar. Let's trek to Alberta!" (That actually *has* happened on at least one occasion. The friend has not asked me to go hiking since.)

There are actually three tops behind my house and the only reason I don't get suckered into summiting them more regularly is because they are all very steep and very far. I forget this sometimes. Like I did this weekend when we put on our snowshoes in the worst ever snowshoeing conditions and schlepped ourselves upward.

I try not to be a condition-oriented outdoors person, but there is a particular kind of snow that is not optimal for snowshoeing. It's the kind that sticks heavy to the bottoms and tops of your snowshoes until you have the ballast of approximately one overfed and overdressed Latvian baby dangling from each ankle. It's the same kind of snow that does not support your weight despite the wonky, wide shoes. Step-sink-hoist.

It was arguably miserable from the beginning, though this did not seem to deter us from the possibility of going to the top of something. Hours later, out of breath and well-aware that the descent would be no easier, we summited and celebrated with some sort of pounded dates in a square shape.

It's amazing what tastes delightful when you're cold and hungry. I've had more than a few delicious, soggy, indeterminable peanut butter sandwiches in the great outdoors. Often, I just eat the bag too.

As we descended from the mountain, the sun set behind the tops of other things. It lit the sky on fire in an explosion of purples and pinks that faded slowly over the next several miles. Headlamps were turned on. The conversation was limited by the swish-slog of snowshoes. It didn't matter. We were thinking the same thing.

A little fresh air always does one good.

The Garden Optimist Emerges
from Hibernation

I WASN'T ALWAYS A GOOD GARDENER. Based on my seed-to-actual-plant ratio, I likely never will be.

Gardening is much like childbirth in that one forgets all the pain and misery, and when the next one comes around, naively charges forward with the same kind of maternal love and optimism.

"Have you been collecting seeds for years?" asks my person, staring at a spread of crop potential that could end world hunger in a single season.

"Uh, no, I just ordered these."

Ordering seeds when my garden is still under two feet of snow adds to my ambition. I have visions of the snow melting and this rich, weedless soil being exposed, waiting to tenderly accept tiny plants. In reality, it is a maze of gopher tunnels and overgrown tansy remains.

Because my kill ratio is so high (seeds to plants, not gophers to gardens), I must purchase approximately 18,000 heirloom, organic, hand-picked, prize-winning seeds. My greenhouse spread of bright packets of Cosmic Purple Carrots and various exotic strains of tomatoes would be the envy of even the gardening store.

I also like to collect climate-defying seeds, as if I would be the first person to successfully grow a northern okra crop or a cashew tree. Visitors assume I am running the 4H gardening club or competing nationally at state fairs. I'd claim success if I could just make my own jar of salsa come September.

Still, these first weeks of seedlings are some of the best and most rewarding, mostly because everything is still alive. My greenhouse fills with little trays of moist soil, and I happily label each container. This is necessary because I cannot tell the difference between a squash plant and a kale plant, and I read in *Carrots Love Tomatoes* that gardening is kind of like planning a wedding: There are some people you don't seat at the same table.

As the seedlings begin to sprout, I hover over them like a helicopter mom, spraying them with my little squirt bottle and chirping about how proud I am of their resilience and determination. I also read that plants have feelings and so I try to nurture their emotional well-being. If they face challenges as adults, like low levels of nitrogen in the soil or rabbit-bullies, I want them to have the tools to overcome those and thrive in their plant society.

I also grow a few things that could survive a nuclear war, like radishes, because it coddles my gardener ego. It's no matter that most of the season, the family is force-fed variations of radish salads they eat mostly out of pity for my efforts.

Inspired by my spread of starts the other day, I got carried away and wondered out loud if I could just be a homesteader and grow our food. I could get chickens and goats and maybe a falcon or something that eats ground squirrels. How much food would I have to grow to make this a financially viable solution for us?

I turned to see my person paling. I don't know if it was the fear of starvation, an undisclosed dislike for radishes, or the fact that I had invested a small fortune in gardening but still spend the equivalent of college tuition at the farmer's market. In fact, I think he'd be less concerned if I just stopped working but took up a cheaper hobby, like knitting.

But then I'd need to get sheep for the wool. Cashmere sheep, of course.

The Obscure Myth of
a Gardener's Delight

IT IS HARD FOR ME TO DECIDE which animal I like least. This is a stark reminder of the unforeseen challenges of adulthood, because I clearly remember as a child being able to refer to a variety of favorite animals, most of which I hoped to one day own as pets. Such as penguins and Shetland ponies. They would live in harmony, as I assumed all creatures did. Like on Noah's Ark.

I don't know a lot of things, but this I do: Noah did not have a garden on his ark. Because if he did, we'd have a more limited selection of animals to contend with these days. He would have booted rabbits, for sure. They are a gardener's least favorite animal, though sometimes gophers win this prize.

Gardening is a skill not much unlike rocket science except I think gardening has more variables, moving parts, and cussing. I used to think one just puts some seeds in some dirt and then things grow. This is true of tansy, knapweed, and dandelions, but vegetables require an understanding of chemistry, botany, and prayer that exceeds most doctoral degrees or direct connections with God.

Every year, I learn another thing or two about what to do or not do in the garden. Last year, I was feeling pretty savvy when I had my soil tested. I'm not sure why, though, because when they sent the report there were a lot of fancy words and colored graphs, and I was pretty sure I needed to start buying fertilizer on the dark web. Instead, I bought dirt from someplace else so my own yard wasn't quite as incestuous. Then the garden store lady said soil needs vitamins like humans do and she thrust a bag of chicken manure in my hands.

This year was the first year my seed starts actually turned into plants. I had carefully selected them from heirloom seed companies across the nation, then sung them lullabies and watered each one drop-by-drop for months with reverse osmosis water that had been blessed by a monk flown in from a biodiverse farm in Tibet. Also, I encouraged them verbally on a daily basis so they would feel confident in their plant being and grow to be robust contributors to their plant communities.

If I can start a seed, I can probably grow anything. Next year, I'll try okra and mangoes. If that goes well, cashew and white sand beaches. Take that, snowbirds.

With global warming, I can even get a little cocky about when to plant in the ground. Around here, we wait for various peaks to be bare of snow, or Mother's Day, or when the first robin hits the window and falls to the ground. I just waited for my bearded companion to irrigate the garden in a true romantic testament to his love and devotion. Some suitors look for dragon scales on a full moon, but I'll betroth myself to a man with a shovel and eight hundred feet of soaker hose.

For days, I systematically transferred my tiny green plants into this rich, moist soil. Hundreds of little holes were filled with water, roots delicately separated, future meals ceremoniously committed to the earth from which they would blossom and nourish a home with an arguably unusual appetite for anything in the cabbage family. It's our German heritage. Then we celebrated and, as if our prayers had actually been heard, the irrigation system *came on when it was supposed to.* This impressed me more than anything because such things remain mysteries to me, like football scoring and Bluetooth technology.

Maybe that is the hidden joy of gardening. Like raising children and personal growth, everything comes in steps, and we don't often know where we are going until we arrive. At which point we shout things in our heads like, "I have arrived!" I do this every time my child says please or thank you without being reminded, actually.

The gods hear that, though. And then they smite me because that is what gods do. They drop a rabbit into my garden one sunny afternoon just after I've admired my neat rows of promise. A rabbit that has apparently been starving for years because in a single two-hour meal, it eats *every single vegetable* I planted. Every pea shoot. Every buttery leaf of Italian Verona Cabbage. Every kohlrabi, broccoli, kale, chard, and most of my soul at the same time. My beautiful garden of perfectly wet, nourished soil and farmer's market envy is now a cemetery of chewed stalks. When I am done sobbing, I have a bone to pick with Noah.

With any luck, it will be a rabbit bone.

Hunting for Morals and Morels

I DON'T KNOW A LOT ABOUT FUNGI except that I like to eat them and that there is some debate on whether they ought to belong to the plant or animal kingdom based on their respiratory system. I did not eat mushrooms at all until I was an adult, working in Italy, and someone served me a plate-sized plant sautéed in butter and garlic.

I would have turned my nose up at the brown mass, easily confused with a cow-patty, but I was trying to impress my date with my worldly palate. While I stopped going to eat with him, I didn't stop eating mushrooms. It just goes to show that everyone along our journey serves a purpose.

Which was exactly what I was pondering as I was out hunting for morels last weekend with my person. He can be easily mistaken for a Sasquatch and had gone missing some time earlier in the hike. He does not have the outdoor prowess of mythical forest creatures so I was mildly concerned that he may struggle to survive in the wilderness. We had already identified some mushrooms, though, so at least he wouldn't starve to death.

There is something primal, therapeutic, and rewarding about foraging for food, and I'm not sure why we don't do more of it as a society. I suppose the risk of poisoning or hallucinating is rather valid.

We as a people have historically hunted, scavenged, and foraged for nourishment. And while one might argue for the benefits of agricultural development, it has created a clear separation between the eater and the harvester. I wonder if that ever-widening gap is serving us as individuals or a society. I suspect the opposite.

Kneeling on the forest floor, the world slowed down. I picked my way from tree to tree and noticed how the different angle of slopes lent to different growth of flora. I had never noticed that the little white flowers of this shape only grow on the north slopes and that the white flowers of another shape prefer the south slope. Though I often run the trail here, I have never noticed the cedar groves, the windfall, or the peculiar patterns of plant growth just off the beaten path.

My mind wandered while my slow hunt carried me over the narrow ridge. There had not been any fires here for a long time, so I would not find some hallelujah field of morels. Every once in a while, I would stumble across one, then hopefully scour the area for more. I started to look for a trend in where they liked to grow. Was it under tree fall? On these clay-like lumps of soil? In the filtered sun or in the filtered shade? My little basket was getting filled enough for dinner, but I was not looking forward to sharing.

With any luck, I would not have to. Nearly an hour had gone by, and I had not seen nor heard my companion. Possibly, he had been eaten by a bear, picked and chewed the wrong mushroom, or fallen off a cliff. Any of those would mean that all of the morels I had would be tossed in a pan of sizzling butter and then right down my very own gullet. Just so no one would suspect that I had anything to do with his demise, I started whistling halfheartedly for him from time to time.

Then it occurred to me that maybe *he* had found the motherlode crop and the reason I had not seen him for so long was because he was crawling around the forest floor shoving morels in his own overflowing basket. I decided the likelihood was high enough that I should look for him in earnest. Then I congratulated myself on having the outdoor knowledge to find my way home or call for help. I also had the ATV keys. None of that was going to serve him, though, and I thought I should let him know to think better before he wanders off in the future. At least bring some moleskin or something.

When we reunited and combined our harvests, we had plenty of food for dinner and then some. We celebrated our find, cleaned and ate some mushrooms, and dried others in the sun for a different day. We had enjoyed an afternoon of solitude and companionship at the same time, relished in the flavors of our find, and had once again been softly reminded of the abundance of nature and our connectedness to it. I can hardly wait for huckleberry season.

When True Love Is Found
in the Firewood

WHEN YOU LIVE ON TOP OF A MOUNTAIN with a precocious twelve-year-old, it's a little challenging to stay marketable. My wool socks are usually full of sawdust, there is inevitably some pine pitch stuck permanently to my elbow, and my hair products include two-stroke engine fuel and garden fertilizer.

Some time ago, I was out splitting wood with a friend, discussing just these challenges. The kind of person who might like to live in the woods, chop wood all day, and hunt ground squirrels probably does not take time to write online dating profiles. We'd make good speed daters though. I'd start every conversation with, "Do you carry a pocketknife?" Because utilitarian relationships make far more sense than anything as frivolous as *romance*.

The kind of history one must have to develop this kind of disordered thinking is summed up nicely in every book ever written on childhood trauma or the *Little House* series by Laura Ingalls Wilder.

"I just want to find someone who likes splitting wood," I said.

Charlie took another whack at a piece of fir and nodded. I wasn't being entirely honest anyway. My fantasy husband also shares an equal disdain for gluten, considers recycling second nature, and would never blaspheme butter or coffee. He would expect me to be late, buy me tools, and know not to call Search and Rescue until I was a good twelve hours behind schedule.

He would have a strange set of hobbies, like repairing fences, burning brush, and greasing hinges. Oh, and refilling my windshield wiper fluid, which is perpetually low because I just assume that some genius invented a way to refill it with rainwater. (Why is that not a thing yet?) He would also think my Home Depot line of credit is an attractive dowry and know that my love language is filing the chainsaw blade and scrambling eggs. And sparkly things, because I'm still a girl, after all.

What I did not learn about love and partnership in my previous forty years is that it has far less to do with commonalities, shared value systems, good genes, passion, or attachment styles than we are led to believe. Much to my Type A dismay, there are no boxes to check. Everything we think we need in another person is merely a request that they accept us as we are (see above).

We often think that a person must be or do in a certain way in order to appreciate our idiosyncrasies. We hope they are as weird as us, as broken as us, as flawed and imperfect as us, as fond of yard work and vegetables. We represent ourselves as our best qualities so that they, too, can check the boxes to ensure we meet the criteria, that the good outweighs the bad. That more boxes are checked than unchecked.

But there's only one box that matters: acceptance. Then you just have to wake up every day and remind yourself to choose acceptance and love even when they suggest putting A1 sauce on a steak. (If you are not sure if you can accept someone yet, just barbecue with them. You'll learn everything you need to know.) Choose love, not *despite* these things, but *because* of them.

When a person who accepts the entire you comes your way, it is obvious. They propose while you're cleaning up dinner in your gym sweatshirt with the kids. And while you cry and lick fry sauce off your finger so they can put a ring on it, they romantically tell you it's already been insured, because they've accepted that you're probably going to wear it rock climbing or bush whacking or wood chopping and they don't want to change a damn thing about you.

Mountain Medicine for the Wee Ones

I HAVE BEEN TRYING TO GET MY DAUGHTER to hike since before she could walk. I hauled her through countrysides in a backpack, then watched her toddle along like squawking cougar bait for some years, and eventually watched her lanky legs (which made up approximately 80% of her body for an awkward few years) make their own way up the trails.

We've had limited success, and most successes have been the result of significant bribery on my part. Which is why it looks like the Dollar Store vomited in her bedroom. I have used everything from candy to toys to encourage a positive trail attitude and merely developed a pathological association between achievement and new dolls for the kid.

As a single mother, I don't even know if it was about her exposure to the mountains, or rather my desperate need to be in them at whatever cost. Sometimes, she wouldn't hate it. There was an age where she understood that camp coffee in the stillness of alpine terrain was when her mother knit the neurological fibers that heal decades of wounds. And that hot chocolate sipped while still in a sleeping bag does the same thing for kids.

There was often kicking and screaming (mostly on my part). Trails were too long. Shoes were too tight. Legs too tired. I had not learned that "positive experiences" reinforce an actual desire to repeat the thing. I grew up with a different version of doing the things: They are joyful mostly because you don't die and are so relieved when they are over. We must *earn* our summits and *deserve* our reprieve. And that is largely achieved through lengthy suffering, minimal whining, threats, and a bizarre genetic toughness attributed to Viking warriors.

When B and I hit the trail this week, she sets the pace. I carry a heavy pack while she schlepps all the good snacks and some strawberry lemonade electrolytes – the secret to hydrating any kid up a hill. I watch her little calves flex in front of me, animal socks pulled up nearly to her knees, oversized t-shirt hanging off her body. She hasn't started caring about clothes yet, but the gypsy orphan appearance means she at least won't be mistaken for wildlife. She tells me stories about a book she is reading – in fact, I think she is basically a live Audible of all the books she's read. Every fantasy book ever written.

There is a moment she waivers. She tells me her toe is sprained, she has a headache, and this will all be too far. We're a mile into an eight-mile day. She sits on a rock, buries her face in her hands. This usually is the part where things get ugly, and I feel obliged to note that her injuries are not real, we have far to go, she's just slowing down the process, and she'll be fine.

But the mountains, and a team of qualified therapists, have taught me a new narrative. It is one of compassion and acknowledgment, of the validity of one's own experience and needs. And dare I say, empathy.

We sit on the rock together and breathe in the mountain air. I offer her something for her headache and toe. We make sure it's moving fine. We eat a snack. We suggest slowing down on those steep sections. She identifies a few wildflowers she's never seen. What she doesn't say, but I know, is that she is leaving to spend the summer with her father and will miss me. She leans on me, and I hold her up, offer her a gummy.

Then she stands up and carries on. The story of dragon slaying continues. She declares that if she were a creature, she'd be a winged mountain goat. Unicorns are the imaginary pets of city girls. The elusive winged mountain goat is much more our style. She chats up a deer she sees. She laughs at the false summit and sings "The Sound of Music" as we cross expansive fields of wildflowers. She asks if we can run on the way down.

And I see that the medicine of the mountains is just as potent for our children. It is even a salve for the injuries we may have caused each other, an opportunity to repair our own story. As we make our way down through the rhododendron-rich forest, heart swelling with gratitude and peace, I am reminded that children are medicine too.

When Hard Mountains Make Soft Spirits

THERE IS NOTHING QUITE AS SOUL PURIFYING as the uninterrupted vastness of nature, or the simple sounds of birds and bees toiling about their morning. Even the occasional flapping of my tent in the breeze could not disturb the sun-soaked alpine views.

But the low hum of something did. I was a little edgy. I had been climbing around the trees the night before, trying to find a branch that could withstand the sheer poundage of our food bag. When two nutritionists go backcountry adventuring, they bring everything but the Vitamix. The local bears were no doubt meandering about the hillside just waiting for the bag to come crashing down, exploding like a piñata full of beef sticks and dried bananas.

"Is that an *electric* toothbrush?" I turn to see Kelly basking in good dental hygiene, wide-eyed, mouth frothing like a rabid hiker.

"Yeff," she said as she handed it to me to show me how small and light it was. This was basically a repeat of the conversations we'd been having for days.

"You don't need two down vests."

"But they are so small and light."

"The heated one with batteries is not."

"But a battery is so small and light."

Backcountry packing is a question of math and comfort. If you want comfort, you probably shouldn't do the math. Kelly hadn't been backcountry yet, and we were planning a girls' adventure down the Selkirk Crest. Of course, first one has to get to the crest – a ten-mile climb out of the valley and onto the ridge. Not surprisingly, my favorite backcountry expert sentence is ". . . then we'll gain the ridge," as if doing so conquers nature, and all things after that are easy. It sounds very Lewis and Clark.

I had a plan, as usual. We'd pack as light as possible, fuel ourselves on powdered coffee, and hike a nearly impossible amount of ridge, animal track, and scree field every day until we made it to Fault Lake to rendezvous with our respective menfolk for a conjugal visit. Because women who have been sweating in dust and rock for days, covered in various wounds from blisters to bleeding scratches, are the epitome of mountain sex symbols. And our soggy wool t-shirts and ripe socks only make it better.

I had recommended Kelly get her bag weight to about 35 pounds or less, but Kelly was on the comfort side of the fence.

"How much does your bag weigh?" I asked a few miles in.

"44."

About four of the pounds were probably apples. Thank goodness, because I forgot one of my food bags in the fridge and was going to have to ration my macadamia nuts. Most wilderness debacles begin with what appear to be minor hiccups that then avalanche into a series of bad decisions and eventually a survival story in *Reader's Digest*. I am convinced that macadamia nuts could solve about half of those problems.

At night, Kelly unpacked her organic, wild-caught salmon dinner meals, blew up her deluxe camp pillow (which looks better than the ones I have in my bedroom), and warmly snoozed with her clean teeth and heated vest. In my head, I calculated how many miles we needed to cover by which time of day to get to various checkpoints by various deadlines.

It was the second day when Kelly gently observed the relentless march might have other options. We were on a trail, heading for a granite scramble, preparing to gain that glorious ridge, when she said, "What if we don't pull sixteen-hour days of treachery and blisters and drag ourselves before dusk into our final camp, dehydrated and bleeding from our knees, exhausted, hungry, and resentful of trees and rocks?"

Obviously, that's ridiculous. There is no other way to back-country adventure. If it doesn't have a certain element of suck and misery, *is it even an adventure?* In any case, that's what I heard, but what she really said was more like, "Hey, wouldn't it be fun to stop at a closer lake and enjoy a slow morning with our people?"

The cognitive dissonance in my head was strong, just like my attachment to the final goal. But Kelly is wise and persuasive and her suggestion that we actually have fun was surprisingly reasonable. I became acutely aware of how little fun I have on these trips. In fact, in the silent moments that followed, I became even more aware of how bizarre my drive for suffering is, how my ego motivates many of my outings, and how often I entirely miss the message of Mother Nature.

When we gained the ridge and slowed down, I could hear the message better. In a single collaborative decision, we had eliminated all pressure for our journey. We could literally wander along the crest at a leisurely pace with all the comforts we wanted, take time to take pictures and smell flowers, and have a wholesome, fulfilling adventure. Without the misery. We could breathe in the sky and be humbled by the beauty that surrounded us. We could maybe even get out of our own noisy heads.

I don't know what it is like when people find God, but I imagine a similar sense of enlightenment. And if that makes me soft, so be it. I could use a little softening anyway. I just didn't realize I could find that in the mountains too.

Family Reunions Facilitate
Barns and Bonding

I HAVE HEARD THAT SOME FAMILIES HAVE REUNIONS. As far as I can tell, a group of biologically related individuals come together to eat potato salad, welcome the drunk cousin, and try to learn the names of the latest offspring additions. They intentionally take vacation days and travel to do these things. And they don't even *build* anything.

In my family, we only get together because someone needs a barn raised or I can't figure out how to hang shingles. Sometimes we get together because someone had a really good-bad idea to do something really stupid-adventurous. Any of these purposes typically end in us overeating salami and crackers, wondering why everything has to be hard, and being grateful that we did not invite the drunk cousin.

The family reunion is at my house this year because I am building a shop. Also, it consists only of my father. Last year my brother came for the reunion and got stung by so many wasps, he just taught me how to hang my own shingles. Working together on a project of this complexity and this much half-inch plywood brings out all the glorious dysfunction one would expect at any other jubilant family affair.

We start out all excited about the potential, and then someone orders the wrong size beams or forgets to pick up milkshakes and the conversation quickly goes from challenging to you're-the-reason-I-go-to-therapy. The only difference I can clearly identify between this and the traditional method is that we don't day-drink because we're operating heavy power tools.

There is a phenomenon that occurs when we interact with our parents and siblings as grown adults. We've had years of experience now as autonomous grown-ups doing grown-up things, raising our own kids, holding down jobs, learning how to run table saws, but the minute I walk onto a jobsite with my dad, I'm twelve years old again.

"Don't drive the nail in that far – you're dinging the floorboards."

I turn my back and roll my eyes because if he sees me do it, I might get extra chores or lose my Jolt! soda privilege. Within minutes, I need to go find some My Little Pony band aids for my blisters or anything else I can do to avoid real work.

Of course, building a shop takes longer than your typical weekend family reunion, if only because my shop is supposed to be large enough to house my bike collection. And potentially aging parents or petulant teenagers. It is a dangerous risk to take – committing to spending that much time with family.

Equally, it's an unexpected gift to see them in their element, being their real person. My dad might be one of the most innovative, skilled carpenters around, and that is something I neither saw nor appreciated when growing up. He just went to work and came home. Working together gives us an opportunity to see different sides of each other and solve the mystery of why people not bound by blood might actually *choose* to spend time with us of their own free will. My dad isn't just my dad. He's a human on his own journey through this life. Fathering me is just one small part of that adventure and who he is.

Which reminds me that I am also not just my daughter's mother, and perhaps one of the gifts I can bestow upon her is to share the other roles I have. I am far less demanding, critical, or opposed to dessert in those other roles. I am a much funner friend than I am mother. And all these things exist simultaneously, but we tend to present ourselves in a rigid, pre-defined role within our families. We are the child to so-and-so, the mother to this and that kid, the cousin who posted bail. But we are so much more, and we seldom have opportunity to share this with family.

Unless of course your reunions are oversized projects lasting weeks during which all the roles of your person are necessary. In fact, I would argue that families should charge straight into that potential dysfunction dynamite and plan activities together similar to corporate team-building exercises. Go on a high ropes course and watch your mom face her fear of heights. Raft a river and plan the logistics with your drunk cousin. Or invite your dad over to teach you how to schlepp plywood up an extension ladder and sink framing nails. Just don't ding the floorboards. You might discover endless new ways to appreciate them for qualities you've never noticed before.

And you'll probably need that in case they move into your shop in a few years.

Rekindling Long Lost Romance

I HAVE FALLEN IN LOVE with a great many people, foods, sports, and rock ballads in my day. I can't exactly say if I am fickle or exuberant with childlike enthusiasm about the world, but either way it's made for a rich life of diversity and a geographically challenged affair with okra.

The thing about finding love is that there is often some lost love along the way (see a string of hilariously mismatched relationships and chia seeds). Through all of those, there has been a single constant romance in my life: running. I have run through a love of plant-based diets, at least one divorce, a post-graduate degree, pregnancy, paleo life, raising a preteen. I have loved running through my rap phase, international travel, trauma, depression, diagnosis, and the year I only listened to Indigo Girls. I even loved running through smoking.

So when running and I had to break up (it's me, not you), the tragedy was felt in every corner of my soul. I nearly had an identity crisis. Not one to wallow, I quickly moved to finding other love affairs. I took up rowing and single leg squats. I tried to learn the banjo. I told myself running was just a stepping stone to other, more fulfilling relationships. I told myself I had to learn to love myself without running's approval and constant acknowledgments in the form of logged miles.

Time passed, and the emptiness in my heart filled with the other things. They were okay, I guess. The rebound relationships of newfound hobbies. But I would often see running off in the distance and pine for the pleasure and pain of its love. I saw other people loving running and questioned their motives. Did they even really love running? I knew I needed to win running back, at whatever cost.

It cost me a surgery and some patience and some hiking. And then it started happening. There was a sort of awkward, intrepid introduction. We had to get to know each other again. It wasn't the roses and dusty toes I had imagined in my head. It wasn't the soft patter of my feet along packed trails, the strides and leaps from boulder to boulder, the wide grin with gnats in my teeth. It wasn't the easy relationship I had once known.

It was work, and it was hard, and my body wasn't even really sure it liked running at all anymore. Some parts of my body threatened to jiggle right off the frame. Also, my shorts felt more like hot pants all of a sudden. I had forgotten the kind of humility it takes to repair damaged and neglected relationships. Maybe running had misled me. Maybe running couldn't be trusted after all. Who is the fickle one now?

I considered throwing in the towel. Then I remembered an interview I saw with Bette Midler where she said the secret to staying married is to never, ever, ever get divorced. This is sage advice. So I kept running. I ran a few miles here and a few miles there. We dabbled in that dirty word – compromise – sometimes walking the hills. Running held out for a little while, but just as I wondered if we'd make it, the grit and grind suddenly gave way to endorphins and bliss.

I remember the exact moment it happened. I had hiked up a long, steep trail. The weather was breezy and cool. The air smelled of wet earth and late summer. I had good memories of running on this trail, even one of me somersaulting down the mountain and managing to bruise every limb and my torso in the process. I turned to descend and broke into a jog. And then, I was running.

It was the kind of run that made me feel like a kid, that erased all my tasks for the day, that demanded I just live free in this very moment, picking my footing and tearing down the dirt path with the ridiculous smile of a woman in love. I floated down the trail on featherlight toes, half panting, half laughing. I might have gone a mile or a hundred. Time and distance had no place here.

And just like that, we were in love all over again.

The Dogs That Heal Us

IF YOU'VE SEEN ME TROTTING ALONG in the forest or meandering around the streets, you've probably also seen my dog (formally known as Freya the Brown Dog) by my side. And if we're out in public or a wilderness area, you'll note she wears a Service Dog harness. It's a contentious subject these days, what with frivolous use of the term, poor understanding of the law, and an inability to enforce the few regulations that are in place.

In Freya's vest, she'll carry some snacks, a wad of biodegradable poop bags, a water bowl, and a bear bell. She also packs our trash out because she inevitably has more pocket space than I do. Her happy companionship and squirrel warnings are not what qualifies her. In her sleek, brown coat, gazing eyes, and relentless tongue action, she keeps me sane. And that's not an overstatement.

To qualify for a "Service Animal" (dog, pony, or something more exotic), one must meet the kind of insanity criteria that gives you real estate in the Americans with Disabilities Act. While the intention of and rights established by this work of legislation are much appreciated, I'm pretty sure most of us would opt out of needing it in the first place. Disclosing that one has a Service Animal is thus an admittance of having a disability, and this comes with a plethora of socio-cultural complications, judgments, and invasions of our privacy.

My entire adult life, I thought my weird seizure things were a case of bad neurological wiring. Something I was born with.

I did not correlate it to my history of abuse, trauma, addictions (mostly cookies and dysfunctional relationships, maybe sudoku), and at least one long night under a big rock. When the specialists suggested I might have some kind of legitimate mental health issue, I did what any avoidant human would do: minimized my history; laughed away the travesties that left me vulnerable, neglected, and prey as a child; then ran a bunch of miles. Only healthy, emotionally resolute people do those kinds of things, so surely I did not really have *the thing*.

It occurred to me later that most long-distance runners probably have *a thing* that drives them to running, and maybe it's not so different from mine.

Ever the over-achiever, I met and exceeded all the criteria for a PTSD diagnosis according to the DSM-5 catalog of mental disorders. Honestly, if you're shopping for one, this particular classification seems readily available and relatively harmless in comparison to some of the others. While current and growing research suggests that various therapies are potentially effective in the treatment of this disorder, for a long time the consensus has been that it's a rather permanent situation. I believe brown dogs – or maybe some white ones – could be the cure, and indeed there are several studies exploring just that.

"Is that a Service Dog?" the kid behind the latte counter asks me. Freya's wearing her label, mostly because I want to be considerate of the other patrons.

"Yes," I say.

"What service does she provide?"

If the questions stopped here, I would be grateful. They seldom do. I'm all for awareness of mental health, but I'm not keen on identifying with PTSD before my morning coffee. Inevitably, someone in line hears me refer to Freya's consistent ability to identify and interrupt what have previously been debilitating dissociative seizures.

You have epilepsy?

No, PTSD.

So she's a therapy dog?

Nope, service animal.

So you are a veteran?

No.

I don't fit the bill for the only seemingly honorable way to have acquired this particular label (I am sure this is no consolation to the afflicted first responders and veterans, either). And neither those heroes, nor other survivors of trauma, or anyone with a disability really wants to explain the validity of their condition in public. Or rehash the history of how they got there in the first place. Also, we'd like it to be easier to get life insurance, thank you.

I am beginning to suspect that dog owners have long understood the universal truths found in the strange, unconditional love of our furry friends. If it counted, I would say that my dog provides the service of allowing me to run for the joy of running. She has been a fundamental part of my redemption and the recovery of my health, as has moving into the mountains where nature's potent medicine patiently works into my cells. She is a constant reminder that it is through connection to and compassion for others that we heal the wounds of life. And you don't even need a diagnosis for that – just a dog.

The One Thing That Will
Change Our Lives

THERE IS A WONDERFULLY OPTIMISTIC APPROACH to solutions these days in the form of singular panaceas. If we could just change *this one thing*, then our entire lives would fall into place, like ducklings behind the unquestioned navigation of their mother.

I find the one thing on a relatively regular basis. As a scientist, I rarely fall for the *one vitamin* that will magically cure all my ailments, but I often find myself a sucker to habits like: Planking daily to promise perfect abs and a happy marriage! Going off caffeine to repair adrenal damage and never suffer insomnia again, thereby making only sound financial decisions and retiring by the age of fifty! Spirulina!

Last year, I went off alcohol for 365 days (it turned into 372). Alcohol gets a bad rap for a lot of things, and rightfully so. It is an addictive substance, responsible for the altered brain chemistry, declining health, and sometimes even death of thousands of humans. My reasons were specific: limiting inflammation and immune suppression while pre- and re-habbing for surgery. I just assumed that everything in my life would fall into place at the same time.

Turns out, I have remarkably few coping mechanisms for things like social engagements with humans I don't enjoy, an incessantly communicative twelve-year old, hard days at work, those blasted ground squirrels, and every time I ever let my future spouse pick out a movie.

Approaching life with clarity makes some things glaringly obvious. I recognized it this morning while I was going for a run.

It was fifteen degrees. It was my fourth day in a row of training. I had survived some sort of workout at CrossFit where we train to leap over rowing machines and then row them. In case someday I might be in a real Viking war where we charge across a fjord to a rival village and then burpee them to death.

I was watching the timer on my watch count down because in thirty seconds or so, I'd have to muster the emotional stamina to run hard up a hill. This is basically the summary of my life. We all have mountains to climb, but I seem to need to set a stopwatch and suffer my way to the top as fast as possible, praying for death or kneecap tendonitis or anything to give me a valid excuse to stop the relentless breakneck pace of my life.

No wonder we want to disengage. No wonder we want to relax, come down, tune out, buffer, isolate, drink Cabernet Sauvignon, watch Netflix, scroll social media, and not miss a day of pharmaceutical intervention. While I may try to set some of the best/worst examples of Doing-All-The-Things-Way-Too-Hard, it is clearly not just me. We are a culture that is going so hard, the only way we can slow down is to check out. By whatever means.

It is not necessarily that we lack coping mechanisms; it is perhaps rather that we have so much coping to do. I am basically half-traumatized by most of my workouts. The pressure to cook The Best Soup at the harvest party gets most of my emotional real estate for a week before. The birthdays I need to find gifts for, the books I should most definitely add to my teetering pile of personal growth literature, the macro-nutrient balanced meals I need to prepare for the week, the sweaters I need to knit before Christmas (2025, because at least we're realistic about some things).

What if we just . . . didn't. The word, as our therapists would say, is self-compassion, but without that tinge of "it's okay if you can't measure up." We can take days off from the gym, pick up a baked chicken, stay home, and slow down. We can commit to fewer things, prioritize that which really matters to us, and stop worrying about how likable or admirable we are. Life seems to be hard enough without us making it harder.

Nearly in tears because the hill seemed to have no summit, I realized there really is a thing that lets everything else fall into place, promises internal peace, and contentment.

Slowing down.

I shifted gears, took a deep breath, trotted over the hill, and noticed the morning sun for the first time. The leaves crunched and stirred under my feet, kicking up the smell of lushness and earth. The field that opened before me was steaming, sending little wisps of fog rising into the backdrop of a blue sky.

And just like that, life didn't seem so hard after all.

One Day in a Snowstorm Mocks
the Fallacy of Convenience

WHEN I BOUGHT MY GRANITE HILLTOP some years ago, my family stared with gaping jaws at me and asked, "Have you gone mad?" If so, I'd blame it on them anyway.

I had grown up much the same way, with the added challenge of poverty and freezing pipes. When my dad saw my funky straw bale cabin, he saw all the impossible work it would take to keep the place up. I'd have to get firewood and split it, and the saw blade would get dull, and then the saw would get stuck. Probably, I'd cut my leg off trying to get it back out. And if I thought all of that yard work was hard before, just try it with a peg leg.

My brother explained the lore of convenience, city life, and plowed streets. I would have to get in the car to go places. No one would ever stop by anymore. I wouldn't have any free time because I would be driving back and forth to town. It's fifteen minutes, depending on how long it takes the turkeys to wander off the road.

My mother, more of a dreamer and optimist, was quiet. She saw the same potential and helped me make my down payment on my dream: the sprawling garden, the quiet afternoons, the cozy wood heat, the knitting.

So this morning when the snow came dumping down and my plans to go for a run and make soup and write my 2020 budget were thwarted by the need to plow, I wondered, "Is this what they meant?" And it wasn't just making the road tidy. Oh no. This dump (which is still dumping as I muse) was the kind that had me checking the chains on the ATV, putting on layer over layer of snow gear, hats, hoods, goggles, expedition-grade mittens, and a soundtrack. It seemed fitting to plow to a little Van Morrison.

As I headed out the door, I grabbed an angel card from a jar on the counter. It read, "Acceptance."

I straddled the ATV as the Brown Dog sprinted laps in the fresh powder. It was just us and the whitewash. We weren't going anywhere today. I canceled my running plans. I realized I'd probably not write an entire new chapter in my book. I accepted that this was my life today.

And it's a fine life at that. Convenience is overrated.

As far as I can tell, convenience is responsible for things like microwave oven cookbooks, binge watching TV, going to a gym to stay healthy, and recommendations on screen time limitations. We haven't really proven to be a species that makes the best use of convenience. It's responsible for trash, the diabetes epidemic, climate change, and PowerBars (which have, at least once, been the reason I swallowed a dental crown which is decidedly *inconvenient*).

As I hammered on the throttle and snow flew into my face, the heavy trees began to shed above us, sending an avalanche over my furry co-pilot and me. If dogs could laugh, Freya would have burst out along with me as we pondered the hilarity of snow coming at us from all directions.

Hours later, fingers frozen and bottom soggy, we thumped our way into the house. The magical world outside seemed unaffected by our roaring back and forth. Silence was restored, and the snow continued to fall. The wood stove was blazing, welcoming us back. The cats came and did figure eights around our feet. I made more coffee on the stovetop. I peeled some carrots for a pot of hot soup that would soon fill my belly. While I cannot speak for my dog, I can say that I felt rather accomplished.

Freya let out a long groan as she stretched out on the floor. I sat down at my desk to wrap my head around finances and grammar. And I sang along:

When no one steps on my dreams, there'll be days like this . . .

The Incredibly Isolating Skill of Doing All the Things

SOMEWHERE BETWEEN HELPLESS DEPENDENCE and sociopathic isolation lies what I can only assume is the collaboration of a healthy marriage. I ought to get more clear on this, seeing as I'm headed down the proverbial aisle in a few months.

Until now, my fierce independence could have been often mistaken for some kind of backwoods brand of feminism, though I would argue any feminizing I did came out of necessity. The last time my chimney pipe clogged, trust me, I called the boy neighbors for aid, but they were all indisposed until it was time to stand below me in the snow and holler advice in my general direction.

In such times, I am grateful for the "figure-it-out" parenting style in which I was raised. It's why I can make such a delicious grilled cheese and tuna sandwich. Or anything with hotdogs as the main ingredient. It is also why I know how to change the oil in generators, make tea from wild plants, and dig my car out of the snow.

And it may also be why I have intimidated partners along the way as they tried to figure out where in my life they might be of use. "I can do anything" had become a kind of mantra that could be easily exchanged with, "Get out of my way." But doing everything is really tiresome. Especially because I don't know how to do everything and I often either have to learn, use duct tape and baling wire, or embrace the kind of innovative thinking that spawns personal injury and ER visits.

What I am coming to understand is not all of us are good at all the things all the time. Thus, it might well behoove us to find someone who is rather good or even merely adequate at those things we loathe or find just plain lousy. In new-age manuals on love and romance, I believe they refer to this as "synergy" or, if you've been in therapy as long as I, "bonding."

My fear of being bonded runs as deep as my fear of being accidentally served decaffeinated coffee. These are basically existential threats. Being dependent on someone is obviously not only *weak,* but also *vulnerable* (the only word dirtier than "bonding").

It would be fair to say that many of us have been in situations where our vulnerabilities were used to inflict harm rather than assure our safety and trust. A booming self-help industry and ever-updating version of the diagnostic manual for mental health is affirmation of this reality.

So when my husband-to-be comes home and says he'd like to plow, or cleans the trash out of my car, or de-ices the stairs, I think, "What does he want?"

"I want no one to break their neck when using the stairs," he would say, as if things were that simple.

It turns out, they kind of are. In fact, far fewer visitors have to sign waivers because of his safety upgrades around the home (and because my dad *insisted* on putting a railing on my stairs). I have also discovered that letting someone else chop wood or clean ashes out of the stove does not mean I am suddenly rendered incapable of completing these tasks and now doomed to a life of grateful servitude. It means I might catch up on laundry (or some other less gender-appropriated task) or take more naps.

While the learning process is slow and grueling, it would appear that relationships are not necessarily a socially acceptable means of indentured cohabitation, but rather a pleasant way to make life a little easier. Sometimes that is in the mere act of commiserating.

Sometimes it's found in thankfulness that someone brought you coffee in bed, just because.

Sure, we can try to do all the things all the time, but why would anyone want to?

Incorporating Roadkill into
Your Backwoods Fitness Plan

I HAVE OBSERVED THAT LIVING IN THE COUNTRY is the easiest, if not most effective way to stay fit, whether intentional or not. While everyone else is out denying themselves pastries and driving to the gym, we country-folk are making ourselves a stack of flapjacks before heading outside to survive.

I support the gym-goers, of course, because moving our bodies is vital to our health and sanity, and treadmills are arguably more safe than any of the terrain I shuffle across. In fact, I'm trying to get the imaging center to give me a punch card so I can get my next MRI for free. It's never a good sign when the radiology staff is on a first name basis with you and asks how the kids are.

The problem with gym workouts is they require a little something called "motivation" that must come out of some sort of magical, mythical pot of psychological ambition. I know some of these people. They set their alarms for 4:45 sometimes. Regular alarms too. I thought they'd at least be using shock collars.

Backwoods fitness is a mandatory sort of do-or-die, chop-or-freeze, shovel-or-suffocate training plan. It also includes all of the best ideas of any other trendy modality out there. The only difference between a burpee and an Idaho burpee is that in the latter, one is holding a shovel and checking under the axle when they hit the ground. My favorite High Intensity Interval Training is firewood: set the logs, chop chop chop until I've dislocated something, set more logs while my heart rate recovers. I should open a gym in my backyard. Some city sucker might just pay me to get my firewood in.

Just the other day I was running in a blizzard, the kind where you wait until the temperature drops and the snow is blowing both upwards and sideways before you decide to gear up for a jog. Winter running is considered "you time" and "self-care" by my family because it's not actually producing anything. In fact, I get to choose the music and eat adult versions of gummy bears. Running in ankle-deep snow while icicles form on my eyebrows and lashes is just conditioning for chore time around here.

As I was slogging up the luxury of a plowed road, I saw a man hiking along the tracks. He was dragging something behind him. I was wondering about his own backwoods fitness plan. Were there kids in a sled? Was he stealing tools from the neighbors? I could see puffs of steam coming off his coat as he worked his way toward the road, and then the stiff legs of a deer carcass in his hands. *Good one*, I thought. *Schlepping a dead ungulate. I know there is a CrossFit workout named after that.*

"Ooh! Are you harvesting that deer?" I asked. Because I live in Idaho, and we get excited about roadkill or train kill, the idea of hides we can tan, and free venison. As I am currently 2-0 with wildlife (one moose, one bambi), I have a wallet full of numbers to call when the next unlucky animal meanders in front of my Subaru.

"Nope," he answered, leaning hard into his next step and grunting as he pulled the large, frozen animal through the snow. It made a soft scraping sound and left a deep path behind him. I was impressed – it must have weighed a couple hundred pounds. His quads must be strong. Not to mention his grip strength. *I need a workout like that guy's*, I thought. He took a couple of breaths and said, "I couldn't make it to the gym today."

It turns out, his motivator was a dog that kept munching on the carcass and coming home to get sick. I can attest that this is the worst kind of dog sick that backwoods athletes have to deal with because whatever end it comes out of, it's full of fur. This has led me to 2 AM workouts where I am running stair laps with a heaving dog and a rug and a bucket of cleaners while holding my breath like an Olympian doing oxygen-deprivation training.

I dream sometimes of the kind of gym where they have TVs and I can catch up on news or a PBS special. I would wear trendy yoga pants and ankle socks as opposed to Carhartt overalls and wool tights. I wouldn't even need gloves or a tourniquet in my workout kit. But it would only be a matter of time before someone says, "Hey, you can't drag that deer around in here!"

The Inevitable Darkness of Being

I KNOW IT HAS COME AGAIN. Sometimes I have a sort of hunch because all I want to do is wear loose sweaters and eat pastries while listening to *The Daily* and wallowing in angst about the state of the globe. But that could just be a Wednesday.

I know it has come when my lunch box pops open on the seat next to me and the task of reaching an entire six inches to close it seems such an overwhelming burden that I let out something between a sob and a sigh of apathy. I decide the gods have chosen to spite me with this necessary effort, and I briefly consider taking the rebellious risk of driving around with my lunch box open because screw them and their omnipotence anyway.

I know that somehow I'll have to brake in traffic, and my lunch will end up on the floor, and the waste, subsequent starvation, and disappointment of dirty salad will crush me with the travesty of it all.

Before this thought process is over, I'm crying and hoping I put on waterproof mascara. I just ordered it off Amazon, no doubt an impulse purchase made in desperation for dopamine. Probably with some sound logic like, "I am unhappy because I don't have the right mascara." It came in a box large enough for a refrigerator. I am single-handedly responsible for the destruction of rainforests in the Amazon now. I wasn't going to cry today, but I live in Idaho, and it's winter, and the darkness has seeped into my very soul. I can't see through it anymore.

This year, like most years, I go through the same motions. I run a hundred million miles. I take my vitamins. I pretend to ski when the sun comes out. I meditate. I go to therapy. I escape to some far away geography where cactus and drought try to dry out my tears. I cut out sugar. And, as usual, I wonder what is wrong with me.

What I don't ever do is simply accept it. I see it as an insufferable inconvenience that does not align with my expectations of myself or my Instagram profile. *If I am doing everything right, how can I feel this wrong?*

This is what I am thinking as I trot down a road on a sun-warmed morning. I've just survived the treachery of attempted trail running where the ice promises a concussion, and I'm trying to feel good. I will myself to do it because I've read enough Thich Nhat Hanh to know none of this matters anyway, and everything is a miracle, and even toast is an "ambassador of the cosmos."

At least it is downhill, I think. *There is no deadly ice here. The snow-capped mountains across the lake are beautiful. I'd probably think toast was a miracle, too, if someone served it to me with a respectful bow every day.*

Also, we all know that if I could find enlightenment in toast, I'd have long arrived at nirvana.

I don't know why I try so hard, actually. Perhaps there is some part of me that knows that when the clouds dissipate, it's nice to feel the difference on the trails, or taste the complex spice of fresh arugula, or to know I am nourished, well-slept, and therapied-ad-infinitum. A midlife woman's version of waking from hibernation is not that much different from a bear's, only I have typically put on weight and rarely get caught rummaging through the trash.

Going through those motions – run, go outdoors, eat vegetables, drink water, read all of Brené Brown's books – keeps me from doing what I really want to do: buy all the athleisure wear and anti-aging products my incessant scrolling has been marketing to me for months.

This year, like most years, just about the time I begin contemplating really bad choices (in footwear, experimental drugs, or hair dye), some inexplicable shift will occur. I won't have to choke back tears when Jason Isbell plays on the radio. I'll laugh when I spill my coffee. I'll not be incapacitated by the task of finding matching socks.

When it comes, I'll breathe the same sigh of relief that my soil breathes when the snow melts, feel the same lightness the trees have when they bud. I can wait, because it is as inevitable as the seasons.

Maintaining Biodiversity on a Socialist Homestead

IT'S THAT TIME OF THE YEAR when I start perusing seed catalogs and planning how I'll nourish the ground squirrel population in my neighborhood. Because I care for the health and wellness of the whole community, it's important to me that I select a variety of culinary delights for the local wildlife.

I don't just want them to be healthy, after all. I want them to be happy, free from student loan debt, and confident in their own ability to contribute to the productivity of the homestead. So far, they seem to be limited to tunneling through rows and trimming the chard down to nubs. My children, not being fans of chard, are satisfied with this arrangement, but I have hopes of one day actually being able to make a meal from a garden harvest. The only thing I've been able to consistently bring inside from my garden has been deer ticks.

Every year, despite the challenges, I make some kind of gardening progress with small successes here and there. I can tell because the ground squirrel population is growing and continuing to look well-fed. Last year, my beau installed an irrigation system and, by September, the weeds were absolutely lush with growth and blossoms. This produced the perfect amount of shade for the squirrels, who were then safe to lounge in the afternoon sun and through owl hunting hours without risk of becoming prey. While we went to sleep with bellies full of store-bought lettuce, at least we knew the squirrels were safe. I imagined them down in the garden like little furry Bacchuses, eating fermented apples with their swollen guts jiggling as they laugh and wipe tomato seeds off their lips.

I don't want them getting fat, though (what with rising costs of squirrel health care). In the interest of keeping them physically active, I adopted two feral cats last year. We may all get toxoplasmosis, but the neighborhood rodents ought to stay pretty fit. Unfortunately, those "feral" cats sleep on my bed most nights, demand organic grain-free food from a dish, and maintain a live catch-outside-and-release-inside mousing program. I'm pretty sure I even saw one carrying a "Feel the Bern" sign last week after I came home from the vet with a pet insurance flyer.

In the interest of learning how to balance my home ecosystem more effectively, I bought myself a copy of *Five Acres and Independence* to go with my copy of *The Ultimate Guide to Homesteading.* The latter is where I learned that most of the trees I'd paint-marked for spring firewood felling were larch, not dead. It is also where I learned everything about wood stove heating that does not seem to apply to my wood stove (which regularly defies laws of combustion and physics). Also, that book suggests that if one sets traps, the squirrels will *go in them,* but I have never, not once, despite creative efforts and a Costco supply of walnuts, caught a single one.

I am thus holding onto the belief that we can all live in harmony on the granite hilltop, though I have absolutely no evidence to support this. What I have is undaunted, naive optimism and the kind of emotional resilience that only years of therapy can produce. And faith in squirrel humanity. Also, I've been reading just enough Buddhist literature to muster compassion for all living creatures. This will probably last me through my first round of seedling transplants. By June, I'll be looking up traditional recipes for barbecued ground squirrel.

Art Therapy for the Poor Prepper

CONTRARY TO POPULAR BELIEF, my solar-powered home, and the size of my pantry, I am not a prepper. In fact, the one time I tried to can my own food, I put butter in the applesauce and nearly killed everyone with botulism. For the longest time, I thought mason jars were just time capsules for food.

"Just scrape the layer of fur off the top. It helps amplify the nutritional value or something." I learned this from my Granny, who regularly served pies from Martha's preserves, only Martha had passed before the moon landing.

If I had ambitions to be a prepper, it would really only be to establish some sort of street (dirt road) credibility amongst my neighbors. Most of them have seven years of grain stored in the spaces of their walls. We all know that when the global food supply gets impacted and I need to hide out from the pestilence, I've got a supply of ground squirrels to get me through even the most biblical of famines. Eventually, I'll get hungry enough to figure out how to trap them.

We only keep accidental food rations around here, but it looks like enough calories to get us through at least one or two kosher holidays and about forty long runs.

"How long can we live on bone broth, popsicles, and sports gels?" asks my twelve-year-old.

"At least until the spring crickets hatch," I say.

While the rest of the consciously concerned world is out there wondering how they'll maintain good bathroom hygiene, our family gets hysterical about art supplies and personal space. I have been testing all the markers in the house and issuing regulations on how much acrylic paint can be used in a day. Imagine my disappointment when an Amazon delivery arrived today, and it was just a twenty-pound bag of organic brown rice.

"We can live on that for a while," said B.

"No, I bought that to weight my training backpack."

When you are a writer and you work from home, there are two specific highlights to every day: school drop off and the secret after-lunch nap (to inspire, of course). Suddenly, my new officemate has various contributions to make to my productivity. Primarily, violin practice and the incessant sharing of toilet paper memes. If my partner starts to telecommute, I'm going all Hemingway and pitching a canvas tent in the backyard, complete with his supply of Scotch. I'll go on squirrel safaris by day and drink by night.

"Can you believe the social angst?" someone asks me at the grocery store.

I have an eight-pack of premium organic toilet paper under my arm. It was made from birch trees that were sung lullabies so the fibers would be remarkably soft and absorbent, and probably infused with probiotics for the bottom-biome. My faith in humanity was restored in that moment, but only because I didn't have to wrestle some soccer mom in yoga pants and latex gloves for it. It's really hard to intimidate or bite people when you're wearing a face mask anyway.

I don't think people are as afraid of getting sick as they are afraid of getting sick of their people. There is some sort of psychological process occurring, and it seems to have pre-ordained steps. It begins with naive ignorance, then followed by sheepish embarrassment at how we preferred the lemon and lavender hand soap to the stuff that works. Then comes a phase of elitist refusal to set foot in a Costco, followed by a passive inquiry into which stores still have short lines or recent supply shipments. Thankfully, Staples was one of them, and they still had sticky notes and felt tip markers.

While so many things seem out of our control, I am finding comfort in the stability of our tiny environment. The pace of everything has slowed. There is something sweet and rewarding about that. I can observe the gradual shift of the season, what pops up out of the winter soil. We're embracing a different kind of routine – something calmer, funner – getting up early to jump on the trampoline instead of rushing out the door. We're reading books, playing games, and writing stories.

"It's about a girl who transports to a different dimension to escape a pandemic," says B as she scribbles in her new homeschool notebook. "She was tired of living on granola bars and listening to her siblings complain."

I am convinced that the lessons we take from the weeks and months to come are not about fear and scarcity, but abundance, grace, and gratitude. And just maybe, we'll learn to keep the best parts as we evolve out of the others.

The Resiliency of Our Children

I TAKE IT ALL BACK.

All that optimistic hoo-hah about connecting with family, reading books more, really developing my watercolor skills. Everything was going great until we ran out of the good food. My journal entries are a step away from just being a pocketknife scratch on a wall.

> Day 14, 2:00 PM
> We have eaten all our chocolate and popsicles. The children have refused to brush their teeth for a week. They are circling the kitchen and making irrational demands. Charlie is sure he saw one carrying a conch shell.

There were a few days in there where we tried to rein them in with our new "We're Schooling at Home!" energy, as if teaching a gaggle of children basic math is more like a hobby than an actual job. If you have ever doubted the leadership and crisis management skills of the professionals who herd our children from eight to three on weekdays, let me clarify: These folks should be in charge of missile crises, wayward dictators, and petulant presidents.

Also, they should be in charge or our children because I lost control of mine on about day four. Last time I checked, she was trying to buy an Army tank with Bitcoin on Craigslist and is looking for hot pink combat boots to match her leather miniskirt.

"Did you do your algebra?"

"Algebra will not save you from the zombie apocalypse, Mom."

"No, but it might save you from the Mommy apocalypse."

I'm not scaring her. She knows that when I run out of coffee beans, I'm just going to wilt into a drooling, mumbling pile of useless desperation.

> Day 12, 6:00 AM
>
> I think the kids might be getting up at night to sabotage my coffee supply. I found charred beans in the fireplace and at least two popsicle sticks. Also, I can't find my credit card, and someone called to see if a forty-foot trailer can make it up our driveway. Strange times.

My vision was much more like when there was a long winter in *The Little House on the Prairie*, and everyone sat around burning their last candle and making beautiful hand-stitched sleeping gowns. I can tell you something, that Laura Ingalls would have been telling a different story if she had to spend fourteen hours a day negotiating screen time.

> Day 6, 9:00 AM
>
> Success! The kids have agreed to complete one math problem after every hour of Minecraft. I don't know why teachers are so critical of video games. They got through ten problems today!

We've taken to spending our time discussing contingency plans that mostly involve Charlie and I barricading ourselves in our bedroom with a box of flares until the children get drunk enough on the last of the chocolate syrup that we can escape during their post-binge nap. We've buried a gallon of it in the yard for when it's time. Instead of sewing, I've been cutting my sheets into strips to braid ropes for our escape. If I see any Barbie heads on forks, I'll know it's time.

Day 1, 4:00 PM
We made a schedule so we can keep the kids up to date on their schoolwork. I'm so grateful for this family time together. It's such a gift to be able to see how resilient and adaptable the children are.

Machines That Go Whirr

I CAN'T CLAIM TO KNOW a lot of certain truths in this life, but I can tell you this: It's highly unlikely I will ever be a cabinet maker.

As far as I can tell, cabinet makers have a lot of special tools. Some of them are scrape-y tools, some of them are shave-y tools, and some of them are pokey. They also use a variety of fasteners. I keep my fasteners, all of them, in a single rusty bucket. I call it my nail bucket, but there are some different things in there, and I'm not real sure what they are used for.

Occasionally, I find the right kind of twisty-pokey tool to stab the fastener into things, and it holds one thing to another thing for a brief moment. It is with this same naive ambition that I requested some pallets from which I intended to build flower boxes. I was slightly deterred when I discovered that measurements and math would be required, but thankfully I am currently homeschooling someone who is adept at fractions and Pinterest research.

I have to do this project when Charlie is not around. This is not new. I do a lot of secret projects when Charlie is not around. Sometimes I involve him by describing the project innocently, as if I have it all figured out. I use a lot of words like "easy" and "simply" and "a few minutes." For a while, I thought maybe he was developing a tic, but I noticed his convulsions mostly correlated to me suggesting that spray foam can be used to fill any hole of any size. In fact, I have some ground squirrel holes I'm going to try it in soon.

Usually, when he leaves for work the next day, I find a wagon with pokey and twisty tools laid out in order from largest to smallest, along with screws that are all the same size and a drill bit that actually has the same shape as the head of said screws. It's like a tool fairy came in the night. Sometimes I think the first aid kit has also been relocated to a more obvious place, but I can't be sure.

I believe that all machines that go whirr have essentially the same capabilities. Some whirr a little this way, and some whirr a little that way, but for the most part, they'll eventually whirr a board in half or lengthwise or at a forty-five-degree angle. After that, it just takes a few bent nails to mostly attach one board to another and you pretty much have a cabinet. If you want to get *real* fancy, I suppose you could engineer some hinges with bailing wire. If there are any gaps, fill them with spray foam.

One of the benefits of living in a straw-bale house built presumably by someone who was on a psilocybin vision quest is that there are no right angles to be found. In fact, they are so rare that building anything symmetrical or at ninety-degrees would rather disrupt the whole Dr. Seuss structure theme I have going on here. It is with this flexible optimism that I set to breaking down pallets for lumber, a project that has mostly just yielded swear words and kindling.

I briefly thought about purchasing some boxes and just pretending that I'd made them myself, but it's really hard to find carpentry with as many bent nails and blood spatters as I would need for that authentic self-made quality. Besides, I have just enough success with the whirring machines to stay cocky.

"You can't make that board," says Charlie. "You need the [machine that goes whirr through the table] or it won't have straight lines." It's cute that he thinks I know what a straight line looks like.

He was barely out of the driveway before I marched into the shop to assess the whirring machines I might use. He has been working diligently for weeks to organize the tools so that I might easily find things for my projects. Right there, at the front of the tool bench, I found all the hand saws hanging neatly on a hook, as if placed just there at a height appropriate for a Norwegian carpentry apprentice. He's so thoughtful.

It wasn't until I finished hacking at a piece of cedar and gluing it to the window frame with spray foam that I realized all the real tools had been safely left out of my direct view and the batteries stored in an entirely different place. But I found them. After I finished my treasure hunt and trim job, and applied a few band-aids, I proudly sent him a photograph of my wonky board tacked to the front of the house.

"You're so good at the things," he said.

Which is exactly why I am going to marry him.

Planning a Backwoods Wedding During a Pandemic

IF YOU'VE NEVER TRIED TO PLAN A WEDDING with a man, let me recommend you choose someone else. Don't forget to invite that man to the wedding, though. Particularly if he's supposed to be your husband by the end of it.

Planning a wedding with your future husband greatly decreases the likelihood that either of you will want to follow through. Everything is exciting and cute until he suggests something like lavender napkins or an industrial handwashing sink, and you start rethinking your original decision.

You won't be alone in this. You'll see his eyes gloss over when you start talking about buying an antique ceramic washing bin for the outdoor sink he's going to build for you with recycled pallets and please, honey, do all the plumbing with that charming reddish piping. Copper? That's cheap, right? I hope so, because those old sinks are not.

Despite having practiced with a previous marriage (or two . . . there was that brief incident as a teenager), I feel relatively inexperienced and uncertain about various matrimonial etiquette. This leads me to panic when people – well, women people – ask me questions like, "Do you have colors or a theme?"

I knew I forgot something! I think as I add it to an ever-expanding list.

I had just about settled on *Frozen 2* when COVID struck, and I had to rethink my entire motif. We're calling our wedding "Romantic Sanitary" and yes, we'll be gifting our guests hand sanitizer and miniature rolls of toilet paper. Some may be attending for the free booze, but my guess is most are coming for the toiletries.

Feeling rather overwhelmed by the prospect of making all these decisions, I asked a married friend how he handled his giant wedding. "Did you hire a planner?"

"We are two gay men, Ammi," he said. "We were born for this."

Which only made me feel like I had a deficit in both gay friends and good taste, though supply of such things is arguably sparse here in North Idaho.

Thankfully, Charlie has focused on that which is important to the male in any wedding ceremony: planting grass seed and organizing the shop. To keep him safely isolated in areas of his strength, I complain nonstop about how stressful all this planning is. Then I delve into the minutia of things like the beautiful gold flaking on this one tea plate I found at the thrift store, and *did he even see the needlework on this garage sale napkin?*

Mind you, I have over 150 napkins, none of them matching, each with unique hand stitching. I'm so busy pointing out petals on Morning Glories, Charlie never has a chance to ask how much I spent on them. And really, that's the whole point.

Hiring a wedding planner seemed rather a fine idea. They could plan everything and just tell us when to show up with our recycled plates and napkins, repeat what someone says, and then buy everyone dinner. Of all my wedding fantasies, that one is my favorite. And the one where my Brown Dog gives me away.

The draw of the details is unavoidable though. Our simple backyard wedding somehow grew into being an advertisement for Pinterest. I'm scrubbing labels off blue jars, deconstructing pallets, and having fits of hysteria because the lupine in the yard might bloom too soon. As if somehow the precise tone of purple has an impact on the veracity of my wedding vows.

Which I haven't even written yet because I've been too busy planning what flavors of cupcakes to order. (Those mini ones, and should I use classic papers or those trendy tulip kind?)

"Charlie! We still have to write our vows!" I worry as I list off all the other things I need to get done first.

"Mine have been done for a long time," he says nonchalantly as he returns to the shop to make sure the hammers are hung largest to smallest or something. "It's really the only thing that matters."

How to Tell What Is Important

I DON'T REALLY UNDERSTAND A LOT ABOUT ASTROLOGY and how the pull of the cosmos affects our lives, but I do know this: Something or other was in retrograde last week. If I had to guess, I'd say the universe was expanding in a direction that promised emotional dismemberment. Like most catastrophic days, they start out soft to make one a little cocky about their coping tools.

"Are you absolutely devastated?" asked my running coach in the morning after hearing that my 100-mile race had been canceled. I've only been training for about 12 months, 2,000 miles, 432 hours, four gallons of caffeinated sugar gels, and at least two really bad blisters.

"Nah," I quipped back. "You don't survive as much trauma as I have without having a fair bit of resilience."

This should be a warning sign to me. Any time I get arrogant, Mother Nature or the full moon or Mercury work their strange ways to reacquaint me with humility. The pattern is so reliable, I only buy waterproof mascara these days.

By midday, I was so confident in my self-actualization, I was going to make amends with every dysfunctional member of my family so I could invite them to my wedding. Why I thought this was a good idea, I'm not certain, but I had at least two cups of coffee that morning. Weddings are not stressful enough, what with promising eternal love and property rights and patience to someone – might as well share the experience with the people you talk to your therapist about.

Not surprisingly, those people are not always on the same path of redemption and gregariousness. My fairy tale of a tearful reconciliation was rather a blathering of insults and outright disgust for the bride and groom, resulting in me contemplating creating a trust fund dedicated solely to psychological treatment (or rehab) for any member of my family. Right now, of course, I'm using all of that money for my own mental health. And wedding caterers. (For every dollar you spend on catering, estimate approximately 25 cents to be spent on premarital counseling.)

Rattled from the barrage of complaints about my character, and still congratulating myself on my resolute calm in the face of challenge, I took my Brown Dog for a walk. She was a little off, probably because, as my service dog, she's an extension of my soul and always seems more aware of my inner turmoil than I am.

It wasn't until we got home that I realized something was terribly wrong with Freya, who curled up and trembled and refused to move anymore. I thought perhaps I had broken her on the 32-mile run we'd just completed. I asked her what was wrong, but she couldn't tell me. By now, she was shaking rather violently, and I was confronted with the horrible reality that I might be losing her.

Loss and the potential of loss brings a different kind of perspective to the things I might consider important to my life. It is not the things that disappoint us or the people that hurt us that really matter. They are mere distractions, opportunities for growth. What really matters are the people (and animals) who heal us. It is the relationships that serve us with kindness and acceptance every day. It is the Brown Dog that taught me compassion and empathy as an instinct.

I lifted Freya into the car and back out again at the emergency vet while my daughter and I cried with abandon. The doctor checked all the right things to no avail. Only when the doctor slid her hands along Freya's curled-up belly and her hand disappeared into my dog did we see it.

"There it is," she said as she pulled her bloody hand out. We both sighed with relief. If whatever that was hadn't killed her yet, she wasn't going to die. We carefully worked to stretch her out and expose her wound. It was impressive by all gore standards. Freya had made a valid attempt to disembowel herself on some large object, impaling her abdomen deeply and separating her thigh from her torso, but somehow missing her organs.

After a cocktail of doggy narcotics, a long surgery, and enough stitches to make any member of my family proud, Freya was back home and sleeping in my bed, sandwiched between my daughter and me. We took turns fretting over her, bringing her water, carrying her where she needed to go.

By the next day, I had all but forgotten canceled races and wayward relatives. Instead, my tiny family, animals and all, snuggled together in a pile of gratitude for each other. The important things fit right in my bed.

You Can Take the Girl out of
the Backwoods

"DO YOU HAVE AN EYELASH CURLER?" asked the woman behind the makeup counter. She has the kind of symmetrical eyebrows that Mother Nature is not entirely responsible for.

I looked at her quizzically. "Is that like a tiny little heated rod?"

I wondered what the solar-powered version of this beauty ritual is. Can I blindfold myself with nylons before bed so I wake up with the right lash curl?

I never really learned how to do the makeup things. Occasionally, my poor judgment will get the better of me, and I'll slather lipstick on my face, giving the impression of a toddler who's been pilfering in her mother's purse. Mascara inevitably ends up on my cheeks by midafternoon, and like most of my cosmetic attempts, could be inspiration for a Dali painting.

But the girls are telling me I need to get with the program because I'm getting married in a week and "for the photographs" it will look better if my "eyes pop." Apparently, makeup wields this magical power. Which is why I was standing at a makeup counter, comprehending only a small fraction of what this woman was telling me.

I listened, because she's clearly never been mistaken for a Dali, then explained my migrating mascara problem. She talked about long lasting mascaras, volume mascaras, foundations versus concealers, and lots of other things that did not make sense.

"Do you use a primer?" she asked. Suddenly, we were in my wheelhouse. *Primer! Of course!* If I just primed my whole face (and lashes), my makeup would stay where I intended it, assuming I could get it there in the first place.

I bought everything she recommended and left the store with a tiny plastic bag worth several hundred dollars. I had so many cosmetic wonders, I could correct everything from a pimple (kindly referred to as "blemishes" amongst these wise experts) to a pirate's missing eye. My groom may not even recognize who he is marrying, which would just add to the mystery and romance of the day.

I grew up in (and am marrying into) a family where everything is about having the right tool for the job, so the practicality of owning things like brow pencils, highlighters, lip liners, bronzers, and eyelash primer is an easy sell. Applying them isn't hard either, she said as she rubbed it on her hand and used words like "swipe, pat, dab, brush" – all things at which I am highly competent, like caulking and staining trim.

Excited by the opportunity to dabble in the experience of appearing a sophisticated lady of aesthetic nature, I stood in my bathroom before a large mirror and excitedly unpacked shiny box after shiny box. Each tiny carton came with a tinier set of folded instructions for things like "sultry eyes" and "sexy beach eyes." I had a hard time choosing the right option for me because they didn't have "forty-something sun-leathered eyes," but I made do.

Here's the thing though: When branching out of my comfort zone and trying new things, they must at least hold up to the reality of my life. So I took my volumized eyelashes and shimmer glow brows and plump coral mouth for a run. In the rain. Seeing as I cannot get through a rehearsal of my wedding vows without crying at the first sentence, this seemed a reasonable litmus test.

Somewhere around mile four, I took a photograph to send to my savvy girlfriends because there was "good natural lighting."

The only thing familiar about the woman I saw was the smear of chocolate on my face from the Lärabar I had just inhaled.

I went home, used some of my forty-dollar skin-safe turpentine to scrub it all back off and returned to my original plan: a fresh gardening sunburn and some cherry ChapStick.

A Wetting in the Woods

ON MY KITCHEN COUNTER, I have a box of little cards with words on them. Every morning, as my coffee is brewing or I'm chatting with my kid about the day, I pull one from the jar and try to decipher the grand cosmic meaning in that particular though random card. On my wedding day, I pulled "Purification."

I was feeling purified already because I accidentally got some gluten and blew past my ambitious wedding day weight goal in about forty-eight hours. I pondered the word for a brief moment before slugging down some charcoal pills with my coffee and considering publishing a guide blog for celiac brides. (*How to write gluten-free vows,* for example.) Then I went about the day.

If you've ever had a wedding, you'll know that such a day is a whirlwind of disjointed interactions, mascara consultations, and crippling anxiety during which people tell you – typically in five-minute intervals – to "stay present" and "enjoy the moment." I tried by going for a run with my brother, counting the number of bobby pins in my hair, and drinking an obscene amount of caffeine.

I didn't really drop into my body until an hour before the ceremony. I was standing in my bedroom, the third-floor tower in my home, staring out the window at the busy bodies and arriving guests far below me. They were weaving between the trees, wandering down garden paths, hugging old friends with words I could see but not hear. Only, *Why did they have umbrellas?*

My head jolted up as I scanned the mountains on the horizon. A thick wall of gray was approaching, an undeniable drenching heading steadily toward my granite hilltop. It was not a spring sprinkle or a squall but the kind of gush that makes me think God has a pressurized garden hose and my ponderosas must look parched.

The people who tell you that rain on your wedding day is "good luck" probably did not just call off their wedding tent rentals because "the forecast looks clear."

When my surrogate mother stepped into my room, I fell into her tiny but fierce arms and sobbed. I cried at the rain, the world, the loved ones who could not or would not attend. I cried for fear of forgetting my vows (not that there was any pressure for the *writer* to be eloquent and articulate), tripping on the rocks, or merely failing at marriage. I cried because over a hundred people ages one to seventy-five were standing in the rain, waiting to bless my union. And they still looked happy, setting soggy envelopes on a soaked gift table. I cried because I had finally come to understand love, and he was waiting for me to descend the steps of our home. And I probably was going to slip in the mud.

"It's too much," I said. "I feel too much."

I cried until tears washed away everything but the love. When I was done, the rain had stopped, and the green mountainside was glistening as wisps of cloud crept out of the canyons. My room cleared. Women scattered out of the house and into the yard to find seats. Someone handed me a bouquet. I heard the strum of a guitar. I took a deep breath of fresh woodland air and stepped onto the dirt.

Stretched before me was an infinite expanse of rock and grass, shining and clean, smelling heavy of dense forest and wet soil. And there was Charlie. And a hundred-some-odd other smiles, but all I saw was his and everything he ever was or would be, and our love and our future and the steadfast rock we were building it upon.

And it was pure.

The Distillation of Good Memories

"Is this the hardest thing you've ever done?" I asked Aubrey who was slogging across loose scree with an expression of exhausted anguish. Ahead of us was another snowfield, although they'd grown less treacherous as we worked our way around the mountain.

We'd started that morning at seven because we'd dawdled and sipped coffee and eaten oatmeal while we worked up the courage to start our adventure. It was 37 degrees and snow-raining. People were walking past us with their skis. The lifts rushed up and down the mountain, disappearing into the heavy clouds that blanketed Mount Hood.

"The trail is under three feet of snow," said someone at the lodge. I wasn't worried. I can get lost even when a trail is visible, so I was prepared with maps. I had backpacked around the mountain before, though this time we were planning on running all the way around it in a day. But things never really quite seem to go as planned. As far as I can tell, that's the definition of an adventure.

We were trotting down the forested slopes in those early hours, the incessant rain pummeling us but not washing away our smiles. Aubrey is one of my favorite outdoor companions because at thirty he's an incredible specimen of athletic ability and adventure naivety. He'll say yes to *anything*. He's also the best backcountry conversationalist I've ever known, a competent outdoors person, and he shares his food – essential criteria for any friend of mine.

I was just settling into the first ten miles, basking in the glow of the endorphins I'm always chasing, enjoying the view of lush, dripping trees, when my foot did a wonky thing. I'm accustomed to my body misbehaving occasionally; however, I have learned that when *it makes noise*, it's probably kind of a bad thing.

I crumpled to the forest floor and practiced my Lamaze breathing, and this rapidly morphed into labor roaring. Having babies prepares you for many things in life – most of them associated with suffering and patience.

I had never sprained my ankle, but once I left it twisted under a rock for so many hours, it since has a sort of superpower of flexibility. Or it did. Now it just hurt in the kind of way that makes me mad. Running around a mountain is hard enough. Why would I want it to be any harder?

I pulled my poles from my pack and muttered something (a compilation of swear words, mostly) to an unusually quiet Aubrey. Then I hobbled onward. I could climb ten miles back to the car or descend five miles toward a well-trafficked trailhead for a ride home. Or just keep running.

Not surprisingly, we somehow kept opting for the latter. Also, I carry some pretty wicked drugs in my first aid pack, which I swallowed down with a caffeinated gel pack somewhere around mile twenty.

There are times in my journeys when I am forced to introspect about the things that drive me. I am unsure of what I have to prove, if anything at all, or why misery and suffering and colder, wetter days with more pain have become some bizarre badge of survival honor.

When will I be badass enough to just sit in an armchair and share old memories? When can I stop making them? Or when can they just be about being a gondola passenger in Venice? I wondered if the pain is what imprints the rest of the memories so deeply into my cells.

I could smell the glacial water of the rivers we crossed. I remember when I first looked up and saw a glimpse of blue skies to the west, and how the sun hit my chilled body and warmed my face and then my bones. I remember how full of gratitude my heart felt breathing in deeply the mountain air. I would forever remember the sound of Aubrey's feet, first light and pattering behind me, then how they slowly began to drag in the dust and rock as the day wore on. Just before the sun set, the clouds broke around the summit, and we saw Her in all her glory for a moment before night fell.

"Yes, this is the hardest thing I've ever done," said Aubrey.

"Congratulations!" I cheered. "Oh how exciting to be a part of a *hardest thing!*" Not everyone is as excited about this threshold as I am. I try to get there a time or two each year.

Suddenly, I understood that these journeys are not about proving anything. They are about discovering myself and some basic wisdom of the universe. Like how all things are relative. Even my lifetime is insignificant in comparison to that of a volcano. And how all things pass, even the suffering. And that we can experience joy, distilled from the minutia of our environment, at the very same time we are experiencing misery.

What parts we commit to memory, now that might be our choice. Maybe that's why I keep going back. Because I already forgot the ugly parts, and memories aren't made in armchairs.

A Rescue Story with a Happy Ending

OCCASIONALLY, I RUN INTO PEOPLE in the forest who are making some bad decisions of their own and I celebrate their optimism and poor judgment, not to mention commonalities. For if it were not for the optimists and poor judges of history, we wouldn't be where we are today. Which is mostly a good place.

This is exactly what I was thinking as I stood in a half squat, leaning into some unidentified thorny bush, arms stuffed into the sweaty armpits of a near stranger as he threatened to tumble down a few jagged rocks and into an oblivion of sidehill flora. In classic form, I was dressed for the occasion wearing a pair of biking shorts and Birkenstocks. This is not my preferred rescue attire – usually I need less padding on my rear end.

Sometime earlier that day, I had happened upon a group of geriatrics. Just about when I was wondering what the proper term for a group of geriatrics is (a gaggle, a gandering, or perhaps a goiter of geriatrics?), I realized they might be in distress. The kind of trouble that church hiking groups get into, riffraff that they are, heading into the wilderness with their ham sandwiches, good intentions, and occasionally unreliable bodies.

Mind you, bodies of all ages can be unreliable, and I've had to have a stern talk with my own on more than one occasion.

Presently, the gentleman I was trying not to drop was also talking to his. "Move, leg!" he commanded, but his legs had done enough moving for the day and, declaring their exercise quota met, were in active protest. Indeed, this charming group of perhaps the kindest (and most grateful and patient) hikers I have ever come across had launched early in the morning on a stroll of good views and good nature several hours earlier.

I stopped to check on them, noting they'd progressed only about a mile during my two-hour ride, when they told me one of their members was struggling. Leaning on the sunny slope was a cheerful gentleman who was well-equipped for any disaster, judging by the weight of his backpack and the pistol on his hip. Except this particular kind, of course. After a brief medical assessment – and breathing a sigh of relief that his ticker seemed to be ticking just fine – I suggested the most common wilderness first aid intervention protocol: "Bring this man some food!"

A flock of clucking women erupted with offerings of everything from ham sandwiches to trail mix, and I'm pretty sure at least one of them was cooking a brisket in her pack. Of all the problems to overcome that day, starving was not going to be one of them. Getting our outdoorsy comrade safely home without calling for search and rescue would be.

I rode my bike down the rest of the trail, moved my car to the trailhead, put on my German backcountry footwear, and headed back up the trail to help the group, who were already making progress with the aid of their younger cohorts. They'd gone at least 1/45th of a mile. We had about 22 more of those to go. And it took us about four hours. We surrounded our patient with stabilizing and weight-bearing arms and carefully negotiated our way down the slope in a cooperative effort of strength and communication until he was safely planted in the front seat of my car.

You can learn a lot of things in four hours, or read all the good parts of a trashy novel, or maybe run a marathon, but it takes a special intervening of circumstances to learn what I learned that day.

First of all, *never* stop doing what you love, even if it is arguably crazy and you're unsure if your limbs are going to cooperate. All the caveats of appropriate risk-taking apply: bring a group of people that can feed you and pray for you and call for help if needed. I am encouraged to know that I can still make dumb decisions after eighty, and I have every intention of growing up to be just like that man. Especially the part where everyone is trying to feed me.

Second, humility and self-compassion turn even the most challenging circumstances into an experience of shared humanity (and in this case, laughter). I have never spent time with a group of kinder, more grateful, more gracious humans. Their positive attitudes, encouragement, and ability to support each other was one of the most inspiring experiences of my life. If you are not surrounded by such humans already, go find them. I hear this particular group can be found getting into trouble most Fridays on the local trails. They are probably accepting new members, although the application process may involve some initiation like schlepping an incapacitated senior citizen through a thrift store or something.

And third, when the opportunity to help others arises, seize it. It is a gift that is often rewarded in unimaginable ways.

The Inevitable Death of a Mother

THERE ARE ENTIRE MANUALS AVAILABLE on how to deal with the emotional fallout of the impending doom of our planet. Some might argue they were written for the snowflakes, but now I hope there are a few extra copies for me.

When I started out on Saturday morning, the sun was not yet up. I was bound for a scouting trip to find a passable route around or over the iconic Lion's Head peaks of the Selkirks. By "passable" I mean that my husband will not threaten divorce if I happen to suggest that route for our next hiking trip.

I refer to a lot of things as "hiking" when they often involve scrambling, scraping, jumping, clambering, scooting, swearing, bounding, bleeding, and clinging-for-dear-life. On this day, I even had to climb down a tree, which I am pleased to report was also done with a backpack, thus qualifying it for inclusion under the umbrella of "hiking."

The trek started with an unforgivable bushwhack. For hours, I forged my way through thick trees and steep slopes of alder and huckleberries. It was one of the most delicious bushwhacks I have experienced, but even the plump, sweet berries did nothing to dull the struggle of the relentless upward push.

The pine needles in my shorts stabbed my rear end with every lunge. There was blood dripping down my right knee, smearing about like war paint with each brush of a berry bush. I had to squint so as not to lose an eyeball on the next pokey branch I would walk into. While not entirely different from other adventures I embark upon, the suffer index on this one was pretty high.

There is an assumption or belief that I must be rather an exercise addict of sorts. There ought to at least be an explanation for a near pathological commitment to this activity level. Sometimes I suspect I even subscribe to that belief, as if I *must* go do these things despite the misery, or worse: I find solace in that misery.

I wondered these things as I scrambled up a granite face, over a scree field, and paused to look at a steep outcropping of exposed rock I would need to follow to summit. I am not a fan of crossing no-fall-zones, mostly because my record for not falling isn't that great. I gathered my calm and my courage and picked my way across, then clambered up the last ragged edges of the mountain to reach the summit.

The smoke had blown in by then, and as I perched on the summit, awaiting my reward, I was instead greeted with a bleak and dismal view of reality.

The world is on fire.

I cannot escape it.

In that moment, I knew that I do not come to the mountains, run miles, get lost, explore, or otherwise for the sake of cardiovascular health or a version of masochistic trauma recovery. I come here for perspective. To be reminded that my problems will come and go, but the mountains and forests remain. They are a source of trust and stability. A constant in a world of inconsistencies.

And now they are burning, and I am the unwitting hospice nurse to an inevitable demise.

I sat there staring out at the khaki sky. I could almost make out the shape of the nearest ridges. I felt sick from the smoke, suffocating in the sorrows of others and a million trees. Unable to see the horizon, I wrote my name in the summit log and picked my way back down the mountain. I felt as though I had emptied my soul on the climb, only to be denied nourishment at the top.

As I descended through the slopes of granite and gnarled forest, the smoke settled in a thick blanket, filling the gaps between trees. I could not see where I had come from or where I was going and knew only that all the determination, grit, strength, and scratches were for naught. I tried to be Buddhist in my approach and focus on the minutia of the tiny wonders of nature, only to be reminded that bugs and chipmunks and children were being scorched by an inferno elsewhere.

Dejected, exhausted, I climbed into the climate control of my car for an escape from that reality, only to drive through it for hours. Even the deer on the roadside seemed disturbed and confused by our dystopian daylight.

When the tears came, I didn't try to placate or discourage them. To be devastated by the tragedy that surrounds us, by the seemingly inevitable death of our mother, by the unstoppable, relentless destruction of the planet, is to care about it. It is a healthy response to this travesty.

And it is through that lens alone, one of care and consciousness, that we can create change.

Self-Worth in the Simple Life

SOMETIMES I THINK I WANT TO BE A MONK, but then I remember that I am far too depraved and egocentric to pursue a career in spiritual growth. So I deactivate my Facebook account instead. Really, it's the next best thing.

As a supporter of *the* media, I have long wrestled with the ethics of social media, even more so lately. And as a middle child with a myriad of self-worth issues, demonstrated by a childhood of stellar report cards and a subsequent love of cocaine (both of which do wonders for the ol' self-confidence), the social media appeals to many of my insecurities even while it fuels them.

The need for validation through others begins, of course, during infancy when we quickly learn that things as simple as babbling and rolling over deliver rewarding responses from our parents. Through various cultural and technological shifts that are frequently studied by sociologists at large, much of our self-worth is now defined by our social-worth, which seems to be the equivalent of what people think of the representative we send forth.

The irony of the columnist does not escape me.

Thus, I set out to explore that which validates me, only to find it had less to do with what people think and much more to do with the tiny acts of self-love and selfless-impact. The latter I fulfill by sitting on my child's school board, where I also fill my karma account and I-was-an-involved-parent account. Selfless indeed.

The truth is, self-worth is experienced when we do things that remind us of it. Like putting my vitamins in a tiny porcelain dish and actually remembering to take them. Or making myself a cup of tea with a rather gluttonous serving of honey and sipping it while I write. Or putting an extra log on the fire because I like it when my house is the kind of cozy the Danish brag about in coffee table books.

I find it in going for walks, buying the softest ball of cashmere yarn, and taking time to interpret Billie Eilish song lyrics with my daughter instead of rushing to wash dishes. Then I find it in the simple act of washing dishes because it means my kitchen is clean for me in the morning.

In the morning, I wake up to a chilled house and wrap myself in a comically huge robe that I try not to trip over as I make my way down the stairs to the fireplace. I open the vent and watch the coals turn to flames, lighting up the clean counters. Even the click of the igniter on the stove or the scrape of the coffee pot as I pull it over the blue flame sounds like love.

Whatever has happened that has driven us to seek our self-worth outwardly is sadly misleading, for the search is an internal one. I have spent decades seeking it in the mountains, in race times, in social engagements and on social media, only to find it diminishing. Sometimes even replaced by anxiety and fear, or worse: competition.

As I sip my coffee, breathing deeply the scent of woodsmoke and percolation, I wonder if my experience and the value of it are diminished because I failed to post it on Instagram, or have I kept something sacred and intimate just that. Not everyone has a right to share these moments with us, and those who do are probably passing the sugar.

Mother Nature and
Other Domestic Terrorists

ON OUR PROPERTY, WE PRIDE OURSELVES on our progressive approach to equal access to, and housing opportunities for, the local wildlife. So long as they stay outside and refrain from becoming domestic terrorists.

Occasionally, they forget this rule, and we have disputes that disqualify me from any monastic ambition I may have. Shamefully, I often find myself repeating the abusive mantra of, "You made me do it" to a number of spiders, ants, and flies before I swat them dead with a rolled-up issue of *The New Yorker*. In this way, I get through the issues way faster than if I were trying to read them.

When I am feeling particularly gregarious, I will research ways to keep these critters out of my house in the first place, only to discover sage but useless advice like, "Keep all cracks and crevices sealed."

My house is literally built around a rock, and like most rocks, it is made up of cracks and crevices. And some chipmunk nests, cat prowling areas, even a bat cave. It's a veritable ecosystem in itself and basically a stone ramp to other vulnerable areas one might expect to find on a straw bale cabin that tries to survive my ownership.

The feral cats, who have grown lazy after eating most of the birds in the yard this summer, seem to lose interest in protecting the perimeter this time of year. Fat and content, they sleep on my bed all day, feral indeed, basking in my overwhelming guilt at having their little ear tips clipped.

They seemed wholly uninterested when I leapt out of bed last week in a middle-of-the-night psychotic episode of wall-banging combined with a bizarre sort of intellectual plea with nocturnal beasts to quiet down. Because some mice have moved into the third-floor penthouse of my bedroom wall.

I had dreamed of little mouse real estate agents showing the place with all its amenities: Great views, out of cat range, some leftover wasp larvae to munch on, and occasionally the neighbors watch *Hamilton* in its entirety. If you stand right here, you can peek through a knothole and feel like you're watching it live on Broadway!

I would probably be less incensed if they were quiet neighbors, but apparently some sort of mouse fraternity has been established about six inches from where my pillow rests. I am *sure* I hear them doing shots while listening to *Eurovision* competitions, or whatever the rodent equivalent of hazing is.

I assume they are frat mice because they seem utterly unperturbed by my palm-thwacking interruptions. I hear them peep a little, rustle to hide mouse paraphernalia, and then carry on as usual. By now, they have figured out that it will take a hacksaw for me to get to them. They rightfully assume I won't march out to the shop for an extension cord and tear out my very bedroom walls just to get a good night's sleep.

This is true. But I did call the exterminators.

In my mountain home, I am mostly happy to be self-sufficient. However, there are a couple of jobs I am thrilled to outsource: anything that has to do with calculating amp-things or watts-stuffs, and the killing dead of varmints.

It is not an easy job to be my exterminator, as I require much assurance that said animals will not suffer. I need a kind of Kevorkian of pest control to come by and play their favorite music while overdosing them on rodent barbiturates. I would prefer these companies have something more like terrorist negotiation training.

They could just coax the mice out of my walls and promise to relocate them to a better area where they didn't disturb anyone. For example, I have a neighbor who likes to use his tractor to put speed bumps on my road, and he's a little hard of hearing. It's a wonder his eyesight is still good enough to see me flying by.

While there is some sense of needless tragedy, the promise of a good night's sleep has provided solace in this difficult time. At least until I have to hire a paranormal specialist (another trade I prefer to outsource) to get rid of their tiny ghosts, which will no doubt haunt me and my consciousness for the foreseeable future.

Managing Husband Resources

THE PRIMARY DIFFERENCE BETWEEN MYSELF AND MY HUSBAND is that he usually knows what he is doing while I mostly just pretend. Also, he is occasionally known to admit defeat or error, whereas I will go to my grave firm in the belief that Ikea printed the instructions wrong.

When one has a husband, they are a resource to be carefully managed. For example, mine went to a school that teaches people how to do building things *and* he has a beard, so I allocate him to everything that is carpentry-related or involves a chainsaw. Also, anything I don't like to do, such as putting fuel in my car, removing stink bugs, or paying off my credit card.

While it may seem like I am doing no favors for the women's liberation movement, I would like to note that I have long been liberated and this is why I know that I don't like running the chainsaw. Also, I still do carpentry work, just not when he is looking. Because he would ruin our marriage by suggesting I actually measure and mark the wood before I cut it.

When my husband starts tinkering on a project himself, I employ a series of avoidance tactics so as not to become an apprentice. We have long established that I make a poor apprentice, as I am far better at giving instruction than receiving it. Also, I'd much rather be knitting or running or making a mess of his tools while he is preoccupied.

So this weekend when he pointed out that our stove pipe had a hole rusted in it, I responded by arguing about the hole, then suggesting the children make fantastic helpers. I have changed the stove pipe before. It starts with one section and finishes with four trips to Home Depot, me cursing on every level of my house, and the inevitable distribution of ash and creosote throughout my living room.

"It's just the elbow piece," he said with the cute naivety of someone from a state known for barbecue and beer.

For the next several hours, I refused to make eye contact or engage directly with the husband. If he attempted to lure me into the conversation, I blurted out that I forgot something in the oven or that the pastor called or my mother died and rushed out of earshot as quickly as possible. All questions were answered with unrelated vocabulary.

"Do you know where the drill bit is?" he might ask.

"The oil in my car is getting low," I'd respond.

I thought it was working pretty well until I came downstairs to discover that we had no stove pipe at all. Apparently, we'd just have to open the kitchen door when we had the fire going or maybe set the kids up with some palm leaves for fanning.

He returned sometime later with several lengths of new pipe. As far as I could tell, he had bought out every hardware store in the county and had enough piping to start his own side business. Of course, none of it fit together.

"Does the pipe look like it is leaning?" he asked.

"Did you eat all the cookie dough?" I answered.

As the day wore on, there was a fair bit of banging, and crimping, and screwing together of things. My husband doesn't swear often, but I knew it was getting bad when I heard him say, "Jiminy Christmas!" right in front of the children. With minutes to spare before he left for work that afternoon, he finally had the entire pipe connected again. It looked kind of like a hamster tube maze running right through the living room. I congratulated him on his engineering, gave him a kiss, and sent him on his merry way feeling rather chuffed at how successful the day had been for both of us.

Until I made a fire.

"Uh, Mom . . ." asked my daughter as she emerged from her room of sacred teenager space, "what's all this smoke from?"

It seems my smell hasn't quite returned, although I was beginning to wonder why my eyes were watering. As the house filled with billowing smoke, we rushed about (probably like hamsters) trying to find the leak, but it appeared that "everything" was leaking. The last time I found a leak in the pipe, I tried to fix it with duct tape and aluminum foil, so this time we just put the fire out.

While my husband and I don't agree on everything, we do agree on this: If we ever win the lottery, we are spending our money on hiring qualified professionals. Apparently, all our pretending isn't getting us anywhere.

Thwarted Homesteading Daydreams

RIGHT AROUND NOW, I START PERUSING SEED CATALOGS. Hoodwinked by their cunning advertising and false optimism, I invest embarrassing amounts of money in heirloom seeds and empty hope. Then I basically hold a family board meeting during which I present my case for The Best Gardening Year with a color-coded planting schedule and map.

They humor me with nods and sometimes even pick out some wacky tomato we ought to attempt. When I leave the room with my row plans and tiny sketches of beets and kohlrabi, I know they turn to each other and have a different conversation about stocking up on Kleenex and sympathy for the inevitable catastrophes that will strike.

I think I get a little smarter every year, but the varmints seem to intellectually evolve just a little faster. One year the ground squirrels will ruin me, the next it's the aphids, and then it's some hot weeks and my poor time investment.

It starts with the eight hundred or so seedlings I put in my greenhouse. Only my greenhouse is like a Dutch oven, and it stunts their growth or scorches them in a matter of minutes. Those that have survived my over/under-watering rhythm will then be faced with the challenge of transplantation. This is where only the most robust varieties of evolutionary stubbornness prevail. And radishes, of course.

This year, I figured I'd save myself some heartache and a solid work week by simply purchasing some starts from people who know what they are doing. I do this every year, only some time in June after Mother Nature, freeloading wildlife, and poor gardening acumen have killed off everything but the bracken. This ought to reduce my budget significantly.

I also need to learn how to reduce the number of things I do, particularly the failures. Mostly, so I can do more things. There is a certain level of things I must always be maintaining. God forbid I ever had a moment where I was not oppressed and overwhelmed by my to-do list. I may end up napping.

Like many things in life, I have approached my oversized garden with oversized goals and dreamy fantasies of hallelujah vegetables, not to mention the omnipotence of self-sustenance. By now, we know that I couldn't survive a month without coffee bean imports and those grease-stained bags of whole roasted chickens. I might as well just embrace it.

By getting chickens, of course.

Every time I concoct some genius idea that is going to relieve me of pressure and simplify my life (or at least reduce my sense of defeat), I am compelled to fill that open space with a new challenge. Thankfully, my husband knows this and has mastered the art of what I call "supportive discouragement."

It goes something like this:

"I think we should get chickens. And fainting goats."

"I like eggs. How are you going to build the coop?" asks husband.

Obviously, I thought the whole reason I had a husband was to answer all those questions for me. Confused and disoriented, I respond.

"I could totally build a coop. Out of a barrel! I saw it in *Mother Earth News*!"

"Yes, Honey, you can do anything you put your mind to."

His ability to avoid putting *his* mind to my grand schemes is impressive if not downright cunning. Also, he never forgets to buy eggs when he is grocery shopping because he knows if he did, I'd drive to the co-op and solve the problem with a dozen chicks. And the owls and coyotes would probably eat them before they ever laid a single egg.

Like childbirth, I forget the misery, and these things never seem to deter me from trying again or trying differently. Gardening and homesteading require a kind of inherent resilience (and naivety) that I most certainly possess. My hope is that these qualities will eventually prevail, and I may some day at least get to enjoy a zucchini that cost me 40 hours of work and $40 of starts.

The dream of celebrating that meal is what keeps me going. I know I'll proudly present it on the kitchen counter with a smug grin.

"How's that dinner tasting?" I'll ask my husband. Before he can even answer, I'll be trying to convince him to let me raise bison.

When Your Husband Decides
to Move In

MY HUSBAND GOT A JOB IN TOWN. The same town I live in. For the entirety of our friendship, courtship, and marriage, our relationship has been based on 48-hour-intervals and social media engagements. Needless to say, I'm panicking.

When he was home last weekend, I meticulously gathered a pile of exotic ingredients to make a traditional Israeli dish. I plucked the leaves of herbs, thawed wild halibut, minced fresh garlic. The kitchen was a cloud of complex scents from mint to turmeric to sumac to cilantro.

In the pantry, there was a fresh pot of elk and sweet potato stew I had made on the wood stove. On Sunday we had fajitas with roasted peppers, cabbage salsa, and rich conversation. My husband stared at me with that blue-eyed gaze of an adoring, satisfied belly. Home-cooked meals are his love language.

I may have given my husband the impression that I cook like that all week, which in turn may have led him to seek out local employment to begin with. Those gas station chimichangas of northeastern Oregon (where he has worked for years) aren't exactly sophisticated cuisine, no matter how much hot sauce you soak them in.

From Sunday to Thursday, I don't have a husband to impress. I basically live on tacos and variations of tuna salad or an entire bag of popcorn. I recognize the mild moral dilemma, considering that I am a nutritionist and all. I escape the guilt of hypocrisy by buying overpriced organic sprouted corn tortillas and touting the health benefits of guacamole.

For years now, I have only had to appear to be an attractive mate a few hours a week through emotional availability via text message, casseroles, waterproof mascara, and a carefully curated athleisure wardrobe. As far as my husband knows, the laundry never piles up, I did not eat a sleeve of gluten-free cookies for breakfast, and I perpetually smell like lavender lotion.

There are a host of conversations we never have because I don't have to share my popcorn in bed most nights. I am considering setting up a secret mini bar behind my hanging clothes where I have pull-out drawers of Toblerone and little jars of peanuts.

Also, and he doesn't know this either, my brown dog literally sleeps on his side of the bed most nights. Under the covers. On his pillow. We've been blaming the hair on the cats for a while now.

Weekend me is a different me. I'm not harried from wrestling a teenager out the door every morning, or from planning snacks and lunches and gym clothes and running clothes and pick-ups and drop-offs and board meetings and clinic hours and a visit to the DMV and eight thousand phone calls, plus personal hygiene and trips to the hot bar.

Weekend me wears an apron and listens to NPR while baking apple cobbler. That woman even *sits on the sofa* sometimes or reads a book. For entertainment. She's well-slept and well-run and well-fed and even showered.

The maniacal Monday-to-Friday version has been thus far a well-kept secret that is soon to be irrevocably exposed.

For a while now, there has been a sort of common discourse about the wonderful impacts of having my husband home all week and the sort of marital bliss we can expect. And while it is true that I won't have to plow ever again on a Tuesday or get out of bed to rid the room of stink bugs (this was in our wedding vows), when he asked me how I felt about his homecoming, I burst out in a blathering mess of overwhelm.

"I don't want to have to cook for you every day! And I can't wear makeup every day and sometimes I smell like yesterday's workout, not lavender!" I cried, as if these revelations would suffice for an annulment.

"Oh good. I don't want to have to cook for you either," he said, because he knows feeding me canned chili would for sure. "Also, I watch YouTube videos."

It was a true test of our marriage.

Thankfully, the conversation ended in a mutual acceptance of the other's weekday person, with a few caveats about needs for space in our newly shared environment. While we may have to play rock, paper, scissors to see who opens the tortilla chips sometimes, at least we won't be texting each other goodnight.

The Trust-Building Exercise of Exercise

For about five months out of every year, I cannot have friends. It isn't that I don't want them, but rather that they find me so boorishly intolerable that the survival of our relationship depends on me flying solo for a period of time.

I call that period of time, "Training Season."

During Training Season, the entire focus of my personal growth and free time is dedicated to the strategic and methodical execution of a training plan for some particular event – or six. If it's not Training Season, I'm dedicated to Recovery Season, which looks exactly the same only I eat more pie and experience more guilt. Somehow, I assume that resonates with my social circle more.

I track my mileage, keep charts on my effort and pace, log elevation gains and fuel consumed and heart rate and sleep patterns and my menstrual cycle. I keep databases of so much data, I often don't even know how I feel until I collate all the information and spit out an assessment.

"Sleep score was low last night," I'll tell my husband after checking my latest technological doohickey of impressive functionality and questionable applicability.

"But how do *you* feel?" he asks.

"It doesn't matter. Only the data matters. The data says I should feel tired, so I am tired."

When you're a precision racing machine, these minuscule details become the foundation of a successful training plan and athletic performance. They are what separate a few elites from the pack, the pros from the amateurs, the winners from the weekend warriors.

The problem is, last time I won anything it was a chocolate cake at a raffle. Had there been a cake eating contest, subsequently, I would have won that too. So yeah, maybe I'm a precision cake-plate-cleaning machine.

What I am is a type-A, research-driven, data-collecting, trauma-surviving neurotic who needs proof for everything. It's exhausting.

When I signed up for this year's 50-mile event, I announced it to my family as casually as I could. It isn't just the hours I am gone training, but the hours I spend talking about training, recovering from training, and snarling at anyone who thinks about taking the last cookie. It is that my world morphs into a ceaseless conversation about the minutia of a topic that has almost no meaning to them but provides a necessary structure to my experience.

If the bizarre collection of information is not going to win me any prize beyond fewer toenails, why am I trying so hard to understand it? For that matter, why do we seek to understand *anything?* This is for any of you with a Garmin or a memory of their fastest mile time or married people or anyone who has ever failed or improved at anything.

Not surprisingly, the answer struck me like a leg cramp somewhere around mile fourteen on a frostbitten day. Actually, it *was* a leg cramp. And no matter what I had eaten or what my heart rate monitor said, it was undeniable.

The answer was *connection.*

I grew up in a way that taught me, like many victims of abuse, how to disconnect. I learned that what I felt or thought I felt was probably not reliable. From "that didn't happen" to "you didn't feel that way" to "it was your fault, anyway." I was taught that I could not trust myself (but ought to trust others). I learned I was deceitful and eccentric. But I couldn't gaslight my way out of that leg cramp.

My fidelity to data is about my mistrust of self and rebuilding connection to my own body. It's about listening and learning to trust it. My elevated heart rate confirms that it *felt* hard because it *was* hard. My fatigue at the end of a fifty-mile week (actually, fifty-four point six miles) is valid, and all the reasons why are in a color-coded spreadsheet. That spreadsheet says it's okay for me to take a nap. My feelings are indisputable truth. And should I, or anyone else, want to dispute them, prepare for a litany of supportive facts.

My friends and family don't need the list, though, which is why Training Season is likely a burden on them. They take my need for rest or scones at face value. It's like a sweet salve of unquestioning acceptance, sometimes referred to as "love."

And while I still struggle to validate whether or not I had a good run if my raw numbers don't say so, I am getting better at believing my body, mind, and spirit when it tells me something. Now it doesn't have to scream so loud or justify or earn or wait. We're developing a kind of mutual respect, an interdependence, a connection.

Someday, I might not even need the data. I might not even need the miles. Until then, I'll see training as a trust-building exercise and listen carefully.

The Unexpected Journey
of Motherhood

OF ALL THE SKILLS I HAVE FELT ESSENTIAL to pass on to my daughter before she launches into adulthood, learning how to pack human waste out of the backcountry was at the top of my list.

Unsurprisingly, it was not even on hers.

"Why did you put a roll of bags in here?" she said as she quizzically pulled out a Ziplock full of granola bars, baby wipes, and biodegradable waste bags.

I didn't answer her until we were miles-deep into the canyons of Zion. Any sooner and she probably would have hitchhiked back to Idaho. Even then, I said something cryptic and wise like, "You'll spend a lot of your life trying to figure out what to do with the messes you make."

Several times a year, I try to impart this sort of tangible wisdom by taking her into the wild on an adventure. Success has been mixed at best. Primarily because she doesn't really like hiking. As a compromise, I asked her to look up the most beautiful places in the world she would like to see. After claiming the Grand Canyon looks "like a crack in the ground," she showed me pictures of Zion National Park.

When B was little, I was under the impression children are just an extension of their parents, and she would learn to love/hate the things I love/hate (Bruce Springsteen, AC/DC). It turns out, children, though small and reliant on daily reminders to change their underwear, are actually *autonomous* humans. They even have

189

their own personalities and everything. Understanding this has been a painful process for me.

When we drive into the north end of Zion, it's hard for me to pay attention to the road because I'm winding my way through a landscape painted by God. I don't know a lot about God, but as far as I can tell, the deity knows how to get color right. The burnt red canyon walls tower around us, topped with the saturated green of manzanita bushes. The edges stand out in crisp lines against a blue sky interrupted only by the early morning glare of the sun.

We finish loading our packs and layer ourselves against a bitter wind. My pack is too heavy, but I heave it onto my body with the stoicism of a determined mother. Every pound I carry is one my lanky-but-taller-than-me teen does not have to carry. Also, something tells me I can't trust her with the food.

"How far are we hiking today?" she asks. "My pack hurts. When is the next stop? Is it snack time yet? Let's just go to a hotel and *pretend* we camped."

I am reminded that going into the backcountry involves a kind of detox period where memories and luxuries and task lists of the outside world still matter. That first day, time and distance seem pertinent. The body protests this or that just to be sure one is committed. Those first miles, she remains a dependent extension of me. She slogs along behind me, complains about the sand, needs reminders to hydrate.

I sometimes wonder why I force these things and why I so often make them hard. I know it is my undaunted optimism and my deep-rooted belief that all wounds past and present can be healed by nature's affirmation that we are part of something much bigger than ourselves.

In the morning I put empty water bladders in a small pack. The rivers in Zion are contaminated now, tragic evidence of climate change. Safe water supplies are limited, and I will run several miles to refill us for the day's hike.

Moving without a loaded pack is freeing, and my feet dance around the red rocks as I make my way down the trail. The sun is just hitting the top of the walls of Hop Valley. I feel my soul awakening from a fatigue of appointments, media, board meetings. I can smell the cool sand. I notice lizards, birds, how time passes here in a peaceful rhythm rather than a ticking clock.

When I return, B is packing the tent, and I show her my method because getting all the parts back into the original tent bag always seems a bit of a puzzle. We set out our snacks, and on this day I learn that my daughter consumes approximately twice as many calories as me, and that I will have to survive mostly on sunshine and black coffee. By noon, she's eaten her day's rations.

While I strategize my parenting plan of motivation, B leaps over creek crossings in graceful strides and begins cataloging her earliest memories of the places we have lived.

"I remember we had a floral sofa in India and I hit my head on the marble floor." She was two then. All her memories of India are told from a height of just-below-the-table.

"My room in Germany had the blue wall that you painted when Julie drew all over it and you turned her pencil marks into a mural of flowers." Those memories are about three-and-a-half feet tall. She remembers children's names, the tools and toys of those years, the layout of our flat, the time she biffed it and skinned her knee, how I lied and said I was holding her bike seat but she'd already pedaled off on her own.

What she does not remember: how often I yelled and ran and ran and ran to be away. How the sound of the liquor cabinet opening caused a panic in me so deep, I trembled in bed and pretended to be asleep. The day we told her we were getting a divorce. How awful I was as a mother.

Those were only my memories. And she is not me.

We commiserate on the long days as our packs seem to grow heavier by the time we reach camp. I teach her how to light the camp stove and not singe her fingertips, and she becomes the official Camp Chef, adhering strictly to the instructions of "twenty minutes plus one for each thousand feet above sea level." I would have just eaten my food crunchy. I learn that B is patient about things that matter to her. They are different from things that matter to me. Then again, she ate all my snacks, and I'm starving.

It occurs to me halfway through the next day that I barely know this young woman. These miles become a journey of remarkable discovery. At home, our relationship consists of logistics: get up, go to school, don't forget your lunch, babysitting pick-ups, homework reminders, chores, I-don't-have-time-right-now, getting to bed at a decent hour.

I learn that my daughter can talk literally for ten hours straight. I listen to her explain in great detail how she will structure her high school education to support her European university goals. Until now, I didn't even think she understood a grading system, much less its relevance.

She explains to me that she'll go to school in Denmark, then shares a plethora of statistics about the Danish social system, environmental consciousness, education opportunities, and happiness rating as contributors to this decision. She's thirteen.

I learn everything, and I mean *everything*, there is to know about dragons on a twenty-mile day during which she provides a synopsis of a fifteen-book series. Not only did I not realize that dragon societies were plagued by the same troubles of dysfunctional families and crumbling healthcare reform, I had no idea my daughter had read fifteen books.

Occasionally, I remind her to pause and take in the view. We slip into a synergized rhythm in our days. She wakes slowly while I breathe in sunrise and watch the steam of coffee rise from my cup. She watches from the tent as my smile spreads with the morning light.

There is a vulnerable part of me that is only witnessed in these places. Like a hero who needs their magic potion, the wilderness is where I come to hear my heartbeat again.

B quietly emerges from the tent, her ever-present beanie pulled over her ears, and drapes her long limbs around me, leans her head on my shoulder. She looks into the expanse of landscape with me and takes a deep breath. I know she sees me.

"I love you," she says.

I realize then that I am falling in love with my child all over again for different reasons than my status as mother. I love her gregarious nature, her empathy, her ability and willingness to articulate emotions. I love that she teaches me new things and random YouTube uses and can deliberate on the usefulness of Minecraft while I wince but am forced to recognize the validity in her argument. I love that through her, I am forced to grow.

The unsung beauty of motherhood is in the reflection of our own self through our children. It comes from a place of unconditional love, an offering we seldom extend to ourselves. Our children watch us through eyes of reverence and wonder as we wobble our way through parenthood, trying to give the impression that we are trustworthy, experienced guides. In reality, I get lost in motherhood even more than I get lost on the trail.

To know my child is to take time to be with her, to watch her unfold her mysteries before me as she explores the world and discovers who she is. To be her mother is to bear witness to my own unfurling as the delicate fingers of her laughter and love and enthusiasm for life give me both the courage and compassion to change.

"I learned a lot about camping this trip," B says as we're driving home through the desert of Utah after covering seventy miles on foot. My feet are gross, and my heart is full. We're listening to a book she suggested as we sip our much-anticipated Frappuccinos. Sometimes, she has the best ideas if I can pause to hear them.

I always thought Mother's Day was about honoring our mothers, but as a mother, I'm starting to feel the day is a celebration of our children and the gift it is to offer them stewardship along their journey. As persistent beacons of love and learning, they unwittingly guide us on our own.

Defining Adventure

UPON RETURN FROM ANY EXTRAVAGANT ADVENTURE, I find myself desperately seeking out The Next Greatest Thing in a textbook method of avoiding Post Adventure Blues. Much of my life has been a sort of rumbling-tumbling fall from fantastic dream to failure to spontaneous expedition to epic catastrophe to missed flight in an attempt to avoid stagnation.

I had not yet unpacked my bike bags from my latest packing trip through Baja as I rolled over and excitedly asked my husband, "Have you ever thought about going to Bhutan?"

He had not.

As far as vacation destinations go, Bhutan may seem a little obscure. Unless of course you love the Himalayas, dispersed population, and hard-to-get-to places. Also, there's a hike there that I *really* want to attempt. It only takes about a month.

My husband and I were friends for years before he asked me out to a meal that did not involve our children and French fries, so he's been well aware of my penchant for buying plane tickets first and figuring out the rest later. I assumed that is why he married me (also, I make stiff coffee). So I was a bit taken aback when he didn't leap at the opportunity to schlepp a pack through high-altitude terrain behind his bride for weeks on end.

He's a pragmatic man and offered a host of astute reasons why avoiding adult responsibilities and spending a fair bit of our retirement (or children's college funds) on international travel might seem imprudent. I felt a petal of my blossomed sense of adventure wither and float to the level-headed ground where mature grown-ups with portfolios, life insurance, and a sense of duty live.

I guess I have to go without him. And accept that he wouldn't know an adventure if it smacked him upside the head.

It wasn't a week later that he came home and told me he was buying a motorcycle (for approximately the price of a hike through the Himalayas). Not only that, but an *Africa Twin*. I don't know anything about motorcycles, but if the word *Africa* is in the name, it has to be for adventuring.

This was perfect! I take a lot of flak for risking my life, but motorcycle riding is statistically as dangerous as being a whaler in 1718, so at least now I could point fingers back. Also, we'd need some better life insurance.

Some days later, he came home from a ride with cheeks aglow, heart pounding, and a familiar peaceful smile spread across his face. I have seen that on him before when he returns from cutting trails on the property, felling trees, or spending the day heaving rocks around to build steps into our terraced land.

It's the same contented and pleased look I wear when I'm in the backcountry, summiting a peak, or winding my way through mountain villages where children wear yak-wool sweaters and carry their pet chickens around impervious to mites or the necessity for shoes. Occasionally, it happens when I am gardening, sipping coffee on my deck, or watching my children play.

Maybe a life doesn't have to be geographically extravagant to be rich and full.

"So, early in our relationship when you said, 'I want to travel with you,' you meant, like, to Phoenix to see your family, didn't you?" I asked.

196

"Pretty much," he said. He was already thinking about his next engineering feat: installing an outdoor water heater for me so I can have a bathtub perched against the granite rocks with a view of distant mountains. Other princesses want dragon scales from a full-moon night. I want hot water between the tamaracks.

It occurred to me as I watched him traipsing around the yard, shaping his land to be just so, building an outdoor chess set for our son, putting bike racks on my car: *I am his adventure.*

Talk about risk-taking . . .

The miraculous and wondrous are *right in front of us* every single day. We don't necessarily need to leave our homes to experience the world, albeit I agree with most of Mark Twain's sentiments on the matter. If we can slow down, pause, for just long enough to look around, we're surrounded by the marvelous, exciting, and new.

Sometimes the grandest adventure is discovering each other.

Accidental Discoveries in Medicine

I THOUGHT MAYBE I WAS HAVING A HEART ATTACK. I know they sneak up on women who least expect it, and as an ultra-runner whose only real vice is an unbreakable swearing habit, the last thing I'd expect to have is a heart attack.

Sitting in the front of my car, hands trembling, heart thumping, lungs aching, it occurred to me that I was having an actual *panic attack*. I was fascinated. Nothing had happened, and here my body was acting like it was under siege.

This had been preceded by several days of increasing anxiety (another new experience). Those days were preceded by me playing Human Science Experiment in my kitchen with vitamins. It's not the first time I've gotten myself into trouble with hippie sauce.

As any sane person would do when in the midst of a physio-logical phenomenon in which one's autonomous nervous system goes haywire, I decided to run it off. I have long-perfected the art of cry-hiking and sob-running. Instead of some mild oxygen deprivation training, I found myself huddled on a dusty patch of trail, sucking wind like a broken church organ, tears streaming down my face.

If I couldn't outrun it, perhaps I could outthink it. I'm a pragmatic woman after all. Nothing was really wrong. I just needed to refocus my mind.

I decided to play a game I've since named "Everything is a Catastrophe" in which I think of anything nice and make a colossal disaster of it in my mind.

My child's smile: Oh no, the dentist referred her for an ortho-
dontist appointment, and I bet that isn't covered by insurance, and
what kind of parent does not get her kid's teeth perfectly straight,
and now I am going to go bankrupt for this cosmetic adjustment
that is just another way the patriarchy oppresses women with so-
ciocultural expectations of image, and we're all going to burn in
hell for our vain, shallow pursuits!

By the time I made it back to my car, the world had burned
in a hundred different ways. I tried other things: a pastry, a
hot shower, a cup of tea, finally ending up on the table of an
acupuncturist. I don't know a lot about Chinese medicine. To me,
it's like if Kung Fu had a medical branch. I was willing to try
anything.

I flopped onto the table while she waxed poetic; the soft
warmth of her voice alone was helpful. She tapped needles in here
and there, a few in my head (I was sure I needed many more in
there but appreciated her optimism), hands, arms, feet, legs. Then
she slid a buzzer into my hand in case I needed anything and left
me to stare at the ceiling.

I wondered if this is how voodoo dolls feel. I took deep breaths.
I practiced one of the eight hundred mindfulness methods I've
learned. I was even almost calm enough to close my eyes when I
saw the spider on the ceiling.

Though a stoic woman, I am afraid of these things: tax debt,
losing a leg, and spiders. And this one was crawling toward the
middle of the room, right above me.

"Hey, little guy," I telepathed in his direction. "Let's just make
an agreement. If you stay on the ceiling, I won't leap off this table
in a flailing of limbs and needles and hysterics."

He paused, so I thought we had an understanding. Then he
continued his creep toward a vent in the ceiling. I tried to warn

him that the metal vent was far more slippery than the paint, then I promised myself I *would not move* if the spider fell.

The spider falling: If he falls onto me, he will probably crawl over all parts of my exposed body and sneak under and into my clothes where he will surely lay spider eggs while biting me with those pincer teeth until I am paralyzed, and the acupuncturist will think it was her needles and never even know I was poisoned by a bloodthirsty venomous arachnid that I will become the parasitic host to, causing the next insect-borne pandemic of spider paralysis!

The doctor came in and asked if my anxiety was getting any better.

"There. Is. A. Spider. Above. Me," I calmly stated.

It took her a moment to make out the spider, probably because it was the size of a chia seed. She went to fetch a broom, leaving me to use the powers of my mind to will the spider away from the vent above me. It steadily pursued its goal, and just as it came to the vent, it fell.

There is a special kind of gasp reserved for mortal fright. It's not shrill or dramatic. It's the quick suck of what is expected to be one's last breath. I heard it once when a fireball engulfed my car on a highway for a moment. And I heard it when that spider plummeted toward my rigid, perforated body.

The spider caught himself mid-air. *Oh! You conniving, sick little creature!!!* I lay there, frozen and certain my blood pressure alone was ejecting needles. He made his lazy way back up his thread.

The doctor returned to rescue me from both, calmly disposing of the spider and giving me a few more minutes to "enjoy treatment" while I catastrophized my bill, needles breaking off inside of me, and bugs.

When I found myself back in the car, I noted my heart rate was normal again, and my palms had stopped sweating. I declared the scientific experiment a success, not only because I would now be able to empathize with patients suffering anxiety, but also because I had discovered the antidote: sheer terror.

Spiritual Growth Through Scientific Experimentation

OF ALL THE ILL-ADVISED EXPERIMENTS one can undertake, switching to decaf is the absolute worst. I consider myself expert in matters of poorly considered sacrifices in the name of science. I have fasted on everything from water to juice to air, run "keto" marathons, and even spent a year living as a vegan. Clearly, my tolerance for suffering is high.

Yet nothing has ever compared to the pathetic misery induced by giving up coffee. Once, when I was growing up, I recall thinking my mother had turned into a zombie. I might have been reading a choose-your-own-adventure book in which every outcome resulted in some kind of plague, but that just made it easier to diagnose her.

For days, she wandered around aimlessly in her robe, grumbling and scowling at us, hair disheveled and the glazed look of someone sleepwalking through life. Occasionally, there was a verbal burst of piranha ferocity that reminded us she was not just the walking dead. She would eventually succumb to our pleas to fire up the espresso machine again (one of the few electric luxuries in our off-grid cabin) and return to her fully functioning human self while we all sighed with relief.

It was silly of me to think I would somehow handle withdrawal any more gracefully than that stalwart woman. I don't even drink that much coffee. Of course, the coffee I do drink is high-octane, could fuel a supersonic jetliner, clean the most stubborn sewer clogs, or dissolve a corpse. Indeed, I attribute most of my successes and aptitudes in life to this dark elixir.

Then again . . . *studies show.* This is my experiment-inducing kryptonite. Any sentence beginning with a claim of research-backed outcomes somehow inspires me to attempt to replicate results in my own body. Though studies showed that rats got more addicted to sucralose than cocaine, and I had to draw the line on that one. I'm particularly adverse to synthetic sugars, and it's probably a little cost-prohibitive.

Studies show that caffeine improves athletic performance but disrupts everything from appetite to sleep to fertility to anxiety. I wondered if coffee makes me afraid of spiders. Turns out, I'm much quicker at stomping on them if I have a cup of Joe on board.

On the first day, I drank a cup of herbal tea. If, when I die, I am uncertain of the consequences of my poor choices in life, I will know for certain by what beverages are offered in the afterlife. Drinking tea is like sipping on a dead flower that lost its soul. Or supping from a puddle of grass clippings. It is the clear beverage of the underworld right next to tomato juice.

I realize an entire population of tea drinkers may be appalled by this statement and I commend their Buddhistic ability to be so pleased with so little. As demonstrated by my arachnid-squashing habit, we've already established I lack spiritual depth. Although decaffing brought me closer, because by the second day I was praying for reprieve. I wallowed in delicious memories of buzzing my way around the property from garden to woodpile to laundry. I struggled through my days with a sort of lugubrious fog surrounding my brain and body.

Life without coffee lost meaning. Conversations were empty. I was still terrified of spiders. I still woke up in the middle of the night and nearly ate the face off someone who suggested "peri-menopause." I was too exhausted by the persistent self-pity to take action.

I was literally sorry for myself.

I can't eat gluten, I don't drink alcohol, smoking is so passé. Coffee was all I had left! Even my fancy Swiss Water Process decaf wasn't filling the void of meaningful ritual.

Ten days later, I was ready to throw in the towel when suddenly I woke up feeling sort of *normal*. My brain worked. Being alive didn't feel like a burden. A kind of order was restored, and I was happy, even giddy about the day. I cleaned the house and organized my office. I smiled while I meditated. I set a personal record on a training run.

A successful experiment is one that provides a useable conclusion, even if it is not the one you expect. Satisfied and overwhelmed with gratitude for the breakthrough, I contentedly made myself a cup of tea and sent my husband a message of love and appreciation. He had been so patient with me these last days.

"I love you, too. I hope it was okay that I made you normal coffee today."

The Environmental Impact of Being an Ultra-Runner

FOR YEARS, I HAVE BEEN LOOKING for a good reason to stop running. Other people I know find all kinds of good reasons: their knees are damaged, chronic shin splints, they are too busy, it's too hot or too cold, they don't like it, it's hard, unpleasant, unproductive, and arguably a waste of time and energy.

While all of that is true for me, none of it has the special ingredients of shame and guilt that *really* motivate me to make change in my life. So I keep running.

For the last several months, I dedicated a large portion of my life to additional miles of mountains. I neglected my family and my garden just so I could stuff a backpack full of fig bars and salami and take off into the woods for hours at a time. When I am training for a thing, time on my feet supersedes all other important things.

It is a narcissistic and righteous form of avoidance, but the scientists and doctors keep publishing studies on the importance of exercise. Extrapolating from these findings, we can conclude that *more exercis*e must equate to *more improved health*. This can be further distilled to: If I don't run all day, I will probably die. Most likely of diabetes, choking on a pork chop, or napping too long.

Thirty-five miles into a fifty-mile day last week, I found myself with the right amount of time and misery to dedicate my mental capacity to finding a valid reason to stop running. Not right then – I needed to finish my race and I had about eight peanut butter cups to motivate me – but the next day for sure I could end my running career.

As I teetered up and over mountain after mountain, I dreamed of setting my trail runners on fire. Perhaps some dramatic gesture would be the end of this insane habit? I shoved a salami stick in my face and cringed at the pain in my heels as blisters drained into my dusty socks. I could feel the liquid seep into my shoe. When a blister drains mid-run, the pain is a temporarily crippling, searing, scalding sort of torture. If I got more blisters, that would be a reason to stop running.

On this day, I whined and winced and gasped for a good mile, glad there was no one to hear the embarrassing display, lest they think I am less tough than I pretend. As I rooted around in my pocket for the next snack, the next two hundred calories to fuel me, I had an epiphany.

During this training season, I have consumed no less than forty thousand salami sticks, eight hundred peanut butter cups, seventy pounds of steak, enough Amish butter to justify my own dairy farm, a truckload of brown rice, a billion gels and gummies, and fostered a taco habit that could feed all of Mexico City for at least a lunch break. And half of the year at least, my avocados are probably imported from Chile.

Being an ultra-athlete is not an environmentally conscious hobby. I might well be single-handedly responsible for climate change just by the amount of dead animal that I consume. The packaged stuffs I fuel on create a shameful amount of waste. The sheer amount of calories I process for months at a time is the product of an American culture of naivety about abundance. I should know better.

When I came crashing into the finish line after 1 a.m., I ate two hamburgers and swore off running. At last, I had a good reason. The best reason. I was going to save the planet with my laziness.

Between naps and potato chips the next day, though, I read an article about famous vegan runners. Then I researched waste-free fueling pouches and homemade gummy recipes. I checked the local store for my favorite running shoes. I learned that I can grow my own sweet potatoes here in North Idaho.

One by one, I found solutions to every problem I had created. As I watched a toenail turn vibrant shades of purple, the swelling in my ankles went down, and the shoes I love went on sale. I gave in.

Back on the trail, I found myself breathing in the smell of the forest in afternoon sun. It bakes like a kind of sweet dessert, the cedar and pine wafting together with the summer blossoms of lupine and wild rose. I forgot about the blisters and the time and blended into nature until I was a part of it again.

I guess I'll keep running until I find a better reason to quit. For now, it is what fills me with gratitude for this planet and keeps me connected to the importance of caring for her. I hear some people achieve this with afternoon strolls as well . . . so perhaps there is still hope for me.

Friendship and Other Manifestations
of Fatherhood

"I DON'T WANT TO BE YOUR FATHER," said my dad.

We were sitting in camp chairs, morning sun warm on our backs, sipping coffee, gazing down the slope of the Sierra de la Laguna toward the distant coast of the Pacific Ocean. Between us and the water was a single, winding thread of thin dirt road snaking in and out of the lush, green canyon for miles. Today was going to be a good ride.

"I want to be my kids' friend," he followed up. I heard the second part, but my heart was still feeling the first.

Months before, I had emailed my dad to ask where I might find ridable trails in the winter, when the dull gray of the season seeps into my veins and coagulates my blood. In the recesses of my blackening brain, I relive a painful history that maintains a fierce grip on my neurology. It is the mark of abuse, rejection, neglect. It is the mark of shame, sorrow, and unworthiness.

There is something about me that my dad has always seen, a kindness and tolerance in his relationship to me even when he could not understand my choices (in particular the reckless, damaging ones). What he has always understood is my need to be outside, to go and go far, to quiet the noise in my brain so I can hear the song in my spirit. And so he responded to my email:

"Come ride the Baja peninsula with me."

The Baja Divide is a bikepacking route that stretches some 1,500 miles from San Diego to Cabo San Lucas, with a loop around the peninsula, crossing from the Sea of Cortez to the Pacific

Ocean. The route might be best described as "arduous," although far more expletive terms were used when encountering miles of deep sand, treacherous rocky descents, ceaseless steep climbs, snakes, tarantulas, and one horror-film worthy night with Kissing Bugs – quite possibly Mother Nature's grossest invention yet.

We met in La Paz with our bikes and two weeks worth of camping supplies. While Dad had ridden both The Great Divide and the Baja Divide, this would be my first experience bikepacking. It offered every opportunity for him to be a dad and me to be a daughter. This is mostly demonstrated by him sharing what he's learned in years of bike travel, and me doing it my own way anyway.

It's a forty-year pattern we'll likely never break, a rite of passage we'll repeat until he's gone and I am left to carry it on with my own children. Then I will suddenly be abandoned to figure things out on my own. I remind myself of this as he hands me various tools while I assemble my bike. He's standing over me and shuffling back and forth, probably waiting for me to make some error he can point out. I am afraid I will grab the wrong size wrench and disappoint him.

I know how to put my bike together, I sigh in my head. And then, *These moments are a gift and not without an end.*

When we hit the open road, the warm sun begins to melt the frigid winter from my bones. We roll past hillsides covered in cacti and wind-swept plastic bags, soda bottles, car parts. The sand is a kind of fine gravel, and it makes a soft, welcoming noise under the wide tires of my loaded bike. The air greets us with desert smells as we make our way into the rugged land of rancheros.

Occasionally, a ranch will have a sign outside that lets us know we can resupply with water and snacks. We lean our heavy bikes on barn doors and walk into someone's garage where I inevitably practice the four Spanish words I know. We sit on the ground outside, drink our cans of mango juice, look at maps, share potato chips. We don't try to talk much. It is a quiet intimacy offered only by time spent together.

When we mount our steeds again, we roll beneath an enormous tree that is filled with the noise of what must be thousands of birds. They are loud and sing an exotic, unfamiliar song that surrounds me in stereo as I ride by. It lifts me up, and I recognize where I am and that this is the justifiable purpose of leaving my children and husband in Idaho. Something in my soul is being purified. I look up to see if Dad is experiencing the same epiphany, but he cannot hear the birds and stares straight ahead.

My dad is deaf, and during my childhood, he was also blind. Like many young parents, his vision was blurred by the oppressive, suffocating obligation of providing for an impoverished family. His myopic view seemed to be that hard work would solve the problems and so he set about doing just that.

He didn't see the abuse for what it was. He did not see, could not imagine, what was happening to his daughter. He didn't see that the challenges I brought (incessant talking, lack of boundaries, a fantastic neighborhood crime streak, risky behaviors . . . the list goes on) were the chaotic responses of an injured child.

Instead, he corrected me, trusted me, and loved me through decades of destruction. When I would confess my latest transgression, I would see the confusion in his eyes – a tired, worried sigh. In good times, he equally celebrated my successes to gently remind me there are many paths I could choose from.

The first time he took me up a mountain, maybe it was a deeper wisdom from his own history. A knowledge that enduring wounds could be soothed from time to time by a different kind of suffering, the kind that gives you summit-perspective. The timeless vastness of the desert offers the same perspective: *You are part of something much bigger.*

When we come down from the cliffs to the green-blue waters of the Sea of Cortez, Dad needs to jump in them. He drops his bike in the sand and throws his shirt as he does a childlike scurry to the waves. He splashes his hands in the waist-high water, some courage-building ritual of his, and plunges into the sea. When he emerges, his soul seems purified too.

"What is the one rule on this trip?" he asks me later as I stand on the side of the road waiting for him. We skip words often because my suggestion to take a left turn inevitably becomes, "What happened on Saturn?"

I shrug. Dad has a lot of rules: always wait at the fork, stop for snacks, rest in the shade. I try not to roll my eyes.

"Always stop for water."

He has a sixth sense for the trickle of a spring, even in the desert. When he finds a pool of clear (or questionable) water, he rinses, splashes, sits in it. It is a non-negotiable and one of the greatest parenting gifts he continues to offer me: a reminder to play. He also stops to trade bikes with village kids, or race them around their neighborhood tracks, narrowly escaping certain impalement by giant cacti.

In those brief moments, I see him for who he is as a person, not only as my father. We fall into a rhythm together that allows space for our differences. I go to sleep early and need solitude. Dad sleeps in and needs coffee. I will tantrum if I don't eat enough during the day. Dad will tantrum if he can't have a milkshake. As the miles roll beneath our wheels, I see how much we are simultaneously alike and different.

"You are just in your daughter movie," my dad tells me as I complain at our latest disagreement, some mapping miscommunication, road rules, unmet expectations, or my most volatile button: criticism from my parents. I was oft-reminded of how exasperating and disappointing I was, how sick, wrong, embarrassing. The need for approval lingers in me like a cancer that refuses remission.

When he is ahead of me, I watch his cadence and his line and try to learn. I want to grow up to ride a bike like him. It moves beneath him like a burro, steadily forging through sandy terrain and over rolling rocks. When he is behind me, I want desperately to be a good rider, to prove I have learned and that I can do the things, a perpetual little girl voice in my head.

Years ago in therapy, I asked my dad if my parents had even wanted me, and in a single tear-filled look he healed some of my longest-festering wounds.

"You are what made us a family," he said.

Ahead of me, Dad's shirt flaps in the breeze. I can tell he is smiling. In the open air, the blue sky resting on the crisp lines of the distant, scorched mountains, there is a gentle acknowledgment of how far we have come. The silence on our rides has given us a new language. Ours is a language of being seen.

I sip coffee from my titanium cup and look over at Dad. He is still so young, still so early in his own journey. I watch him take in the expansive view. He cannot hear the bells of the goats, so I tell him they are echoing down the ravines, as though a gypsy parade might emerge from the trees at any moment.

To share these days together, to see the value of these sweet exchanges, is how I sew myself and my frayed understanding of family together again. It is also how I come to understand what he means about friendship. Ours is not a relationship of obligation, but appreciation, and of a love so constant, it will forever be my guiding light.

Much like his distant red taillight as he blazes a path ahead of me on this road of discovering ourselves and each other.

The Accidental Buddhist

BEFORE THERAPISTS AND SELF-HELP BOOKS and life coaches and memes, people were left to pursue personal growth with the unregulated, irresponsible method of "life experience."

This haphazard means of gaining wisdom was mostly used by previous generations. A widespread cultural shift toward vanity and the visceral has the newer generations spending the first few decades of their lives ambitiously pursuing self-actualization through yoga poses and signing bonuses.

In the early evening temperatures, the sun dipping behind robust ponderosas, I sipped my sparkling water while my companion jingled the ice cubes in her wine glass. At 91, she's got it figured out.

"I climbed one hundred and forty stairs today," she says. Her coffee is weak, and her wine is diluted. Her mornings begin when she wakes up, and her days end when she feels like going to sleep. She eats "what she likes" and she occasionally wins a nickel at bridge club.

"How is it," I ask carefully, "to grow old in this way?"

I am wondering if it is imprudent to discuss mortality when someone is on the edge of theirs, but something tells me she knows things I can't find in a book.

When you spend time with her, you'd think her life had been an easy one because nothing much seems to bother her. She grew up in Wisconsin (quite possibly the most easy state), went to school to be a teacher, worked until she retired. She built a house

214

on the Deschutes River in the eighties with en vogue floral-print wallpaper, pine cabinets, and blue carpet.

Then she spent forty years watching birds and gardening. She eats Danishes for breakfast, reads crime novels one after the other, and stares bright-eyed through her gold-rimmed glasses out over the river.

She tells me she has three rules:

One, when she gets stressed out, she slows down. There's no need to rush about and make a mess of things. Just slow it down. (I pay about $100 an hour for this same advice from a trained therapist.)

Two, breathe. With this, she purses her lips and sucks in a deep, fierce breath through her nose, eyes closed, belly rising. She rests her knobby, wrinkled, knowing hands on her abdomen as it lifts. When she is quite satisfied with this, she opens her eyes and slowly, fully releases her breath. "Qi Gong," she says. She took lessons at the senior center.

Third, she avoids toxic people. Simple as that. Steer clear.

Her life was as full of adversity as anyone's. When she was young, she fell in love with another woman. To keep the secret, she bought the house next door, helping her raise three children from a safe distance, supporting her through the slow, cancerous death of another. She watched her unsung love survive a heart attack, then tolerated her Egg Beaters and margarine for another thirty years.

When her partner died, she ransacked the house and cleaned the drawers in a systematic purging of nearly sixty years of a shared life. She said she didn't want anyone to have to clean up after she goes. But in a picture we rescued, she's kneeling next to my grandmother smiling, their pinkies intertwined.

Her wine is now more ice melt than grapes, and she sips just as contentedly on that. Her silver white hair is alight with the last rays of sun. The river roars past us with its constant crashing against the rocks. I cannot see how any life can be fuller than hers. I want to ask her if she meant to become a disciple of the Dalai Lama or if she's just an accidental Buddhist.

"I thought of a fourth one!" she starts. I look at her expectantly.

"It's none of my business anyway. And that one," she says triumphantly, "has been the most liberating."

Raising Future Conservationists
and Other Hopes

I KNEW SOMETHING WAS OFF in the first mile of our climb. I had a big breakfast in preparation for a lengthy summit, but I was well into my snacks before breaking the tree line and still feeling wobbly. I assumed the mosquitoes had drained too much of my blood supply.

When my daughter was six, she climbed South Sister with me in a two-day effort motivated by Sour Patch Kids and the promise of a new Barbie. This is where I learned the power of bribery in the Great Outdoors, a useful parenting skill when the lure of achievement itself is not enough. At fourteen, it would take fewer dolls but more candy.

Volcanoes are often a good way to break a child of the are-we-there-yet habit. They can see right where they are the whole time. You're there when you reach the top and then you can start your sunbaked descent into the cloud of ravenous mosquitoes below. What I love about being in the wilderness is the constant potential for discomfort.

It makes the Mediocre Indoors that much more delicious.

We brought my brother along for motivation. Any signs of weakness would be latched onto for years of ridiculing. As a matter of pride, I kept quiet about my growing desire to vomit on my feet. Altitude had never bothered me, but today it was. Even my lanky daughter, now taller than me, was comfortably making her way up the zigzag of loose rock, rattling off conservationist considerations.

I wonder if there comes a time when age catches up to us and we lose tolerance for suffering. This is likely what is generally referred to as "wisdom" amongst alumni. I trudged silently up the scree, heart racing, wondering when I could transition to a recumbent bike and those chair yoga classes. The writing was on the wall.

The summit that day was surrounded by thousands of butterflies, orange and brown, moving in patterns like flocks of tiny birds. They lifted off the pitted rocks and floated on the breeze, then landed again together on exposed stone between patches of snow. There were no flowers this high, nothing to bring them here except perhaps the view. I was glad to know we have something in common with butterflies.

I watched my daughter and brother converse as we made our way around the rim of the crater. He's a father now, too, and it has brought a softness to him that is endearing and wonderful – a reminder that children can heal wounds we don't know we have. They teach us empathy and playfulness and a thousand other things bludgeoned out of our brains by multiplication tables.

A few days later, I blazed down Interstate 84 toward the Sawtooths for another adventure, but I had not recovered from the climb. I had the growing sense that my body was no longer mine, but a vessel for another purpose. Perhaps the volcanoes and alpine trails were not its priority.

Because class and sophistication have long been bred out of my family line, I discovered the cause at a truck stop where I purchased the usual contraband (beef jerky, kombucha, chewing gum, a mealy red apple) with one exception: a pregnancy test.

Moments later, I sat on the grass under a tree, Mack trucks blazing by with Amazon Prime deliveries, Brown Dog frolicking with stranger poodles, staring wide-eyed at my future.

When my trail runners hit the slopes of the Sawtooths, it was with a lighter load and at a slower pace. I packed more food. I promised self-compassion and stopped to linger over views, flowers, falls. I wore the kind of smile that comes from an overwhelming inner joy.

Though just a tiny embryo, it was already imparting the gifts that only children offer, a reminder that we are but a small part of something that began before us and extends long after us. We can merely hope we bring honor to our own brief moment.

And, of course, to raise carbon-neutral kids who have the same visceral familiarity with volcanoes, the smell of old-growth forests, and the soft sound of rich soil under their feet. If we are to have hope, it is found in them.

On Loss, Grief, and Love

LOSS CAME TO ME ON A MONDAY MORNING in a bloody smear that could not be misunderstood. I gathered my heart from the floor as the trembling began and prepared myself for the unavoidable freight train of grief I could hear chugging toward me. It sounded like my heartbeat.

The gentle recommendation, upon seeing the barren landscape of my vacating womb on a black and white screen, was to go home and rest. My determined, ripe body would soon realize what was happening and give up. I left with a Ziplock bag of feminine hygiene products large enough to absorb a city park water feature and a prescription that would leave me wallowing like one of Lucretia Borgia's lovers. First, though, I needed to run.

"No running for two weeks," they said.

"Right," I thought.

Grief, they say, is not linear. Mine is a four-mile loop that passes a prepper's yurt, a decaying moose carcass, and endless fields of wildflowers.

Tears hit the wooden porch floor in wet stains as I crumpled over my running shoes, desperately clinging to dreams that were no longer mine to own. I climbed the hill behind my house, doubling over time and time again, overcome by the kind of sadness that makes the body retch and heave.

A neighbor drove by and paused to congratulate me on my pregnancy. I cried into the passenger window of his Lexus while he tried to divert his eyes. Miscarriage is not for the faint of heart.

It is also a silent and lonely loss for many, a catastrophe of internal shames and external justifications. We tell women they are part of a normal statistic, they ought to keep trying, stop trying, eat better, adopt, rest more, and generally take responsibility for the incompetence of their bodies or shriveled-up ovaries. Partners rarely get honorable mention in condolences, helpless as they are anyway.

I took the poison and lay in bereavement of the intangible, the not-yet-become, the imagined. When my body was done writhing, my heart finally broke. There was not enough space in the walls of my home for my sadness, and so after a week, I turned to the only panacea I know: the mountains.

"I need to see the world from the top of something," I told my husband, whose shirts are all soaked with my snot now, and who knows Mother Nature's medicine.

With a flaccid, empty belly awkwardly loping over the top of my shorts in a humiliating display of my failure, I sniffled my way up a trail. The dark tunnel of trees opened up with each mile until we were walking in full sun with the world spread before us. With every step, something knit together the frayed edges of my heart.

So many families have navigated this path, but so few speak of it. I have been gifted with a community of celebrators from the very beginning of our journey, and those who shared our joy are now sharing our sorrow. At every turn of our process, we have been met with kindness, generosity, and understanding.

In our grief, we have never felt more loved.

Sitting on the weathered stones of a timeless peak, this truth permeated my lungs like the fresh autumnal air. I remembered all the prayer flags in Nepal, strung across the ridges, waiting for the wind to carry wishes to those who manifest them.

I sighed gratitude into the breeze. Thankfulness for these months and weeks of expectancy and every delight that came with it. Gratitude for a momentary reprieve from crippling nausea. And a deep, humbling appreciation for every kind word, blossom, and hug that has reminded me of the beauty of shared human experience.

And as I drew in a filling breath, chest expanding like the horizon before me, I let a little hope fill the empty spaces once more.

A Garden That Grows More
than Vegetables

AUTUMN. THE LEAVES ARE TURNING hues of gold and red. The sound of the wind rustling through them has a subtle crispness to it, different from the soft and lush rush of the summer breeze.

It's that time of the year that pumpkin spice everything emerges on menus, our sweaters move to the top of our drawers, and I at last harvest the inadequacies of my garden efforts.

But I do it with pride.

The broccoli, both purple and green, stands nearly four feet tall. No matter that it never *broccolied*. The aphids seem to be enjoying it just fine anyway.

There are three pumpkins – or squashes – that grew large enough to be a meal, but now appear to be a kind (scallop) that one eats before they resemble petrified wood, which is seldom found in recipes these days.

The thirty-six tomato bushes produced approximately $36x10^{14}$ tomatoes each, which is fortunate because no one in my family actually likes tomatoes. They do add a lovely bit of color to the yard. Now that the frost has come, they drip from the dead bushes like tears of abandoned marinara sauce.

There were a few unidentifiable peppers, two successful eggplants, and the beet crop this year was delightful. We ate at least six, and only three were mistaken for radishes. The kale continues to be indestructible by wildlife or our digestive systems.

The marigolds, planted to deter critters, successfully choked out enough of the vegetable crops that no deer or ground squirrels even bothered perusing the rows as they'd have more luck finding something edible in the wild. The long-term plan is to discourage them with scarcity, or perhaps they've just taken pity on me.

The plum tree ripened on a Thursday when I was not home to pick them. The apples grew to the size of the pumpkin/squashes and fell heavily from the tree while still tart. Those will be sauced and used as gifts for friends who ask me to serve on any nonprofit board in the coming year.

Still, there is a sweetness to the ritual of shutting down the yard for the season. The lawn was mowed a last time, the desolate and neglected flowerpots moved aside, the badminton net taken down, the firewood moved and stacked.

The garden will be laid to rest for the fall and winter, and true to the nature of such seasons, I will sink into the regenerative and amnesiac magic of rest. By January, I'll be thumbing seed catalogs in an annual ritual regarded as "Misplaced Hope" by even the most optimistic friends.

Admittedly, from time to time, even I feel discouraged, but something always redeems my efforts. This weekend, it was a child from the city. The real city: downtown L.A. Her hair fell in perfect little coils at the back of her neck, bouncing when she ran through the rows of sagging greens.

She reached up for an apple.

"You have to twist them like this," she said as she instructed me on proper apple-plucking technique.

Her apple popped off the branch, and she caught it in both hands and held it to her chest.

"Then you have to catch it like this," she said, demonstrating the delicate movement as she cradled it in her little arms.

She rolled the apple over and looked at it. Quality control.

"There's a bug," she said, flicking it off with her finger. "What kind of bug is that?" She watched it crawl over her pink-tipped cowboy boot, a gardener's staple.

"A black one with pincers," I answer, wondering myself. "In Latin they are Blackoneous Pincerilia, but I don't know the colloquial term." The trick with four-year-olds is to always sound confident.

"Colloquial . . ." she said under her breath as she set the apple in the bucket.

The sun reflected off her stray blonde hairs in the evening light. She tromped over the strawberry patch, poked at a slug, and pointed at a dead leek blossom standing like a giant dandelion.

"I wish I could pick that flower," she said.

I snipped it off and handed it to her. She stared at it with wonder, then shoved the whole thing around her nose and took a deep breath.

She took the blossom back to L.A. with her. If those moments are all I ever harvest from my garden, they will be enough.

Finding Meaning Amongst the Gale

THE FIRST TIME MY GRANNY WENT TO SCOTLAND, she went by way of London Heathrow, rented an RV, knocked a mirror off before leaving the airport, and spent a month seeking out her roots. She came home with a shag tapestry of a bagpiper that hangs in the foyer like a coat of arms and no less than a thousand stories (or the same story told a thousand times).

I grew up spending summers at her home in Oregon, where she spooled threads of a family history that would be woven into my understanding of what we belonged to. Her maiden name had been Spurlock, but perhaps as a penance for her decision to divorce my grandfather in the early sixties, she never reclaimed it. Instead, she reminded me constantly that I am not just Norwegian.

"You know you are Scotch-Irish too," she said with a stern look. Her family had immigrated to Canada and then later to America, then California like everyone else during the Dust Bowl. Being Scottish was the important part of that, but in the photographs of her long and lean father and her stout mother Lovie, one can only detect how bothered they are by the obligation of holding still.

Granny belonged to whatever clan had her favorite colors. The plaid fabric, still in its original wrapping in the hallway closet decades after that trip, was green and purple over muted darks. Others were red and black. More than the bagpipes and the kilts, Granny loved the Border Collies and their trainers. She taught herself how to whistle in the crisp commands of the herdsmen, though her penchant for wayward rescue dogs of questionable brainpower never allowed her to use them.

The second time Granny went to Scotland, it was in an old amoxicillin bottle, her faded name and a decades-old prescription date barely legible from years of wear. Like a treasured stuffed animal or blanket, the bottle has been dragged along on any adventure of merit. She's been in glove boxes, rafting dry bags, Ziploc bags, old film containers, on the top of Kilimanjaro, across the Strait of Magellan, over the Cascades, through the Grand Canyon. But it was always Scotland she wanted to return to.

Our desire to belong to somewhere or someone seems an integral part of our social fabric and our identity. In the case of a fourth-generation American, it is a placebo distilled from haphazard family trees, prejudice, and a scapegoat for obstinance. It is an ancestral home we seek, something we feel we may always return to, should this place lose its welcome. It is the forever-longing song of the immigrant.

I came to Scotland to find a different kind of ancestral home. I came to breathe the same air my grandmother had breathed, feel its earth beneath me, familiar to my spirit somehow. I needed to understand why she wanted to belong here. Because there is not a drop of Scottish blood in our DNA.

In her defense, our English-Irish parts are almost equal to our Norwegian parts. And for some time in America, it was far easier to be Scottish than Irish, and no one in California could differentiate between the brogues anyway. This is the story I make up because there is no one left to tell me otherwise. When our people pass, they take all the answers to all the questions we never took the time to ask. These are among my few regrets in life.

If being Scottish was a state of mind, I wanted to find that state.

I did not know if I would find it in the moors or the highlands or deep in the Loch Ness with the other myths. Or perhaps in the people who are bothered neither by wind nor rain nor anything at all that I could identify.

We drove across the country from east to west, which only takes so long because the roads are narrow and my husband had to pull over occasionally to let his blood pressure recover. We crossed the bridge to the Isle of Skye and made our way to a small stone house on the shores of Loch Snizort. It is not a lake, but rather a bay that faces the impossibly wide horizon of the Atlantic.

The stone house has a place in the history books. Bonnie Prince Charles dressed as a handmaid and was rowed across the water to hide from the English in the boathouse in the 1700s. In the nearly three hundred years since then, the place lost a few stones but had been so expertly built, it was recently restored in one of those renovation projects that ages even the most dedicated optimist. I couldn't help but stare at the stones and wonder about the hands that first placed them here. *What or who did we have in common?*

Hundreds of years before the house was built, my Nordic ancestors rowed their way through the Hebrides Islands. They dropped sheep anywhere grass was growing so that upon their return journey they would have an abundance of food. Some stayed. Maybe we were that kind of Scottish. I stare out the windows at the hillside where white sheep never seem to be moving but are always in a different place. Like their shepherds, they are not bothered by the weather.

"The neighbor's herd lost over sixty sheep to the eagles last year," says Trevor. Trevor owns a croft (the Scottish word for farm) on the shores of another loch (the Scottish word for lake). He is a squat man with bowed legs and the kind of wide stride one gets from years at sea. Before he settled here to raise sheep and give wildlife tours and be a fishing guide, he was a captain on a herring boat (I assume this detail, not a lot of other kinds of boats exist in the Hebrides). So the sheep may be bothered by the eagles at least.

"They were hatched in Norway and raised on fish and lamb," Trevor says, "so they got a taste for it." The pair of released eagles now stun the full-grown sheep by hitting them in the back of the head on a fly-by, then swooping down and helping themselves to a fresh meal. The eagles are protected, so nothing can be done about the matter. Soon, they'll hatch chicks and teach them how to kill sheep too.

"It's evolution," he says with a shrug, giving human intervention a free pass.

We've come to this croft because it is one of the few places that raises sheep for wool. Most of them are for eating. I approve of both, but today I want to learn about the Hebrides patterns. Being a fisherman, Trevor pulls out his sweater and shows us the details. There is a painting of a magnificent horned ram on the wall. The wool for this sweater was from that ram.

"My wife knit this for me," he says, "so you see the cable has two strands, not one. This is so when the gentlemen come to port, the ladies know who is taken." Mothers will knit their sons sweaters with a single stranded pattern to let the women know he's looking for a wife.

The sweaters are made with wool that has not been washed of its lanolin and knit in a tight stitch so as to repel water. Every sweater tells a story: If not from which exact village the sailor comes, then at least the island. His sweater has a bar for his island and an anchor because he's a captain.

"There's only one captain on my island, so if I wash ashore, they know who it is."

There is purpose to the mundane and the minutia here. It is as though sentimentality and meaning are put into all tasks. The seed stitch pattern of the sweater, the colors and pleats of a kilt. They are the love letters one wears so they do not forget to where or whom they belong. I pledge to finish the sweater I have been knitting my husband for several years. And to learn that double-strand cable.

I ask my husband to leave me on the north cliffs of the island on a blustery day so I may make my way home. Wanderers are allowed to trespass through the farms so long as gates are left as they are found. In the distance, I have seen a ridge that calls to my compulsion to see the world from the top of places. I have an unspoken belief I will see the answers from the right vantage point.

I pack Granny in with my snacks and give her a pat as I trot up the trail and into another world. I am sure a dragon will fly or a Viking ship will sail by, but this is a land of primordial history so old, there are dinosaur footprints on the shore. What part of this was in my grandmother's blood and bones? She didn't even like lamb.

As I wind my way upward through the cliffs, the views open up to a landscape of grays and greens, vertical faces topped with iridescent grass. The sea spreads in infinite directions before me, washing into the blue of the sky with a muddled line of mist. The sun is my only defense against the ceaseless wind. It blows through my hood, my hat, my hair, and into my ears with a constant rumble.

When the trail ends, I keep going. A patch of tourists grows tiny behind me as they curiously watch me climbing into nowhere. I cannot explain what I am looking for, that I struggle to belong to a family who denies my memories, and cannot understand where to belong if even the ancestors my grandmother promised are not mine. If they asked, I would tell them I am looking for my story, even as I write it.

The ground beneath my feet is a spongy soil that absorbs every step with a forgiving bounce. My tracks and those before mine are no match for this wind-battered, water-soaked bushland. I cannot see where I have come from or where I am going.

It doesn't matter, really, because where I am in that moment is where I ought to be. Far in the distance there is a dark wall of clouds rolling in from the southwest. They are bringing rain by the afternoon, but for now they just grow taller, not closer. The ridge sweeps softly to the west in an innocent grade, toward hills spotted with sheep and white houses that look like they might be toys from a train set. To the east, the grassy edge drops in cliffs that tumble downward then spread like spilled paint in a flat, green puddle toward the sea.

For hours, I battle the gusts and climb, but the only thing that hurts is my face. For as long as I have been running (or staggering) against the gale, I have been grinning. I belong to the mountains, this much I know.

When I come crashing through the front door in a mess of mud, banana peels, and wind-chap, the first drops hit the house from a horizontal angle. It is blowing over 40 miles per hour now. It rains sideways into the stones for the next 24 hours. We watch the water rise and fall with the tide and how the waves crash in dramatic white explosions on the rocks across the loch. The birds ride the air with wings spread, hovering motionless outside the window. The house does not so much as tremble.

The light in Scotland is like no where I have been. The sky moves by so fast that time on land seems to slow down. Only the colors change. Like the sheep and the people, the landscape is also not bothered by the weather, the news, war, progress, disease, or apocalypse. Stone walls move for nothing, not even millennia. Mangled trees shudder imperceptibly, but they hold their windswept tilt regardless of the incessant breeze.

And then I understand.

Maybe it wasn't the people Granny found kinship with. Maybe it was the country. It was the stoic soils of a sea-bruised shore that patiently waited for the tide to recede. It was the trees that bend to the storms, but remain steadfast in the ground. It was the storm clouds that bring far off promises and carry them to the north. Scotland was the temporary home of dynasties and dinosaurs, migrations and myths, a station at which history rested from time to time to leave its mark. It was the sense that we belong to all this.

For a moment, I felt closer to her than I ever did when she was alive.

My husband bought me a sweater as obvious as the shag tapestry in Granny's house. It was made from Trevor's wool. I wore it as I picked my way across the black rocks exposed by the low tide. Strange sea creatures clung to them. They seem as old as the rocks. The dismembered skeletons of boats lay caught between them. The sky turned a churning gray, and the howling the Scots call "fine weather" was dying down to a breeze that only threatened to peel your jacket off if you forgot to zip it.

I held Granny in my hand. Every goodbye feels like the first one and the last one. The craggy, snowcapped ridges of the Cuillin Mountains blazed white in the distance. Their sun would be our sun in a moment, but for now the clouds parted only enough to let thick beams of light shine on the water, as though a lighthouse were perched in the heavens. It's guiding the next gust to the shore.

When it came, I opened my palm. A million white grains shivered as I uncurled my fingers. It is possible to love more even after someone has gone, possible to grieve them even as we come to know them. And it is possible to belong to somewhere by choice or understanding. We just have to listen to our heart as it calls us home. Sometimes it is hard to hear over everything else.

Suddenly, in a spray of dust that disappeared over the water, she was gone. Maybe Granny wasn't Scottish, but she could become part of Scotland. And now part of me would belong here too.

Disappointment and
Other Ways to Happiness

TYPE A, PROJECT MANAGER FOLK LIKE MYSELF prefer color-coded, scheduled, measured approaches to securing happiness in life. I know this is the way to do it because I see it on Instagram.

This yoga pretzel headstand, this planner, this Zen-like meme about forgiving the people who bulldoze over me, the trails I could-should-would run, and most definitely, this handmade leather purse from an artisan shop in Portland, are all part of the path to contentment of the soul and release from The Great Want.

My calendar is a bludgeoning of joyful pursuits. It is an hourly compartmentalized prescription of the things humans ought to do to *be* happy. So on a fall Sunday afternoon as I checked off my to-do list and noted that I did *all the things*, I blinked out the window in disbelief.

"Why am I not happy? I literally did all the things!!!"

I knew something must be missing in my equation. Perhaps I was stuck in what author and habit-scientist James Clear refers to as "The Valley of Disappointment." This is when you do all the things all the time, but you just have to be patient for the returns on your investment. It's a kind of religious faith I've not excelled at.

Dissatisfied, I baked organic, gluten-free pumpkin bread sweetened with maple syrup and fattened with happy chicken eggs. Aside from being the most righteous bread ever, it was also delicious. Belly full, something was still amiss. Probably I needed bigger pants.

Unable to find the thing to make me happy despite how many pairs of leggings I own, I set about searching for what was making me unhappy. Was it the dead stink bugs in the corner? The chores my kids did not finish?

Outside, in the rain, my husband was working and looking disturbingly happy. He was bundled up, and I could hear the music of his joy across the yard: saws and hammers. He had left the house hours earlier without comment. The banging and drilling were less alarming to me than when I catch him with the hedge trimmer.

That hedge trimmer definitely makes me unhappy. Only to be superseded by the flame-thrower that leaves cubed shrubs charred by overzealous flames. I swear he goes out there and pretends to be Ironman or something, slice-scorching his way across the property like a landscaping superhero.

Disgusted with his apparent pleasure, I wandered out to spread my malaise.

"What are you doing?" I asked, arms crossed over my chest.

"Making a cupboard for your water heater," he said, his blue eyes twinkling. He was even using recycled wood.

I suddenly realized that I had not actually exercised on that particular day, and this must be the reason I did not feel overwhelming contentment and satisfaction in my soul. I immediately put some serious banjo music on and rage-rowed 10,000 meters. If you angry-exercise, it burns the bad fumes of bitterness probably.

Grunting as I pulled furiously on the porch, I saw my husband driving his truck to and fro, wandering around with wood on his shoulders and a carpenter's pencil in his teeth. Then I saw the steam rising from the yard.

I have always dreamed of having an outdoor bathtub. When you live off-grid on solar-powered well water, the common approach is to build a wood-fired solution. But Charlie has been running hoses and moving rocks and cutting wood since he gave me an on-demand water heater for Mother's Day.

Note: When you find someone who knows how much you love propane heaters *and* earrings, marry them.

I sprung to my feet and ran into the soggy yard to find him filling a bathtub with hot water in the middle of our forested acres, surrounded by the gold-red hues of fall.

I squealed with delight and ran back into the house where I had been stockpiling bath salts and bubbles for years in anticipation of this very moment. Reappearing with a cup of hot chocolate, a thick bathrobe, and the fuzziest slippers I own, I stripped and dipped a toe into the water. The warmth spread up my body like the smile across my face.

I sank into the water, kicking and splashing in the suds like a child. My husband left me there, floating in the open outdoors.

The noise of my mind quieted. The wind blew through the larch trees, caught the leaves of the aspens, and sent little gold coins to settle on the fluffy suds around me. I poked my toes out to feel the cool air on them, then greedily sank my whole body into the water.

Across the valley, low clouds settled onto the deep green of the mountains. A cat slunk through the field. For a moment I stopped doing and embraced *being*.

And I was happy.

Acknowledgments

MANY INNOCENT BYSTANDERS WERE INVOLVED in the making of this book. Mostly friends and family surreptitiously invited to partake in various adventures, poorly conceived ideas, or carpentry rescue projects with the full-but-undisclosed intent of writing stories about them later. To those who have suffered blisters, bloody knees, late-nights and all-nights, hitchhikings, tears, monologues, or the various other blessings of being in my inner circle: Thank you. You are what make stories worth telling.

Additionally, I have forced my writing on many of these people, often with the explicit request for admiration and validation. They have all indulged me. Particularly Jon and Liz and Chris, but not Larry, who has a penchant for opinion – popular or not – tempered only by his wife Eileen's graciousness. Thank you. You have made me a better writer and human.

My gratitude goes to Rich Landers, who overlooked my unpolished words and gave favor to my voice, and Eli Frankovich, who is still burdened with my Idaho grammar. And to *The Spokesman-Review* and *Out There Outdoors*, whose stalwart commitments to journalism and community are examples of the importance of both.

And especially to my husband and our children, who partake and patch me up with inexhaustible good humor. I love you.

About the Author

A POPULAR COLUMNIST for *The Spokesman-Review* and *Out There Outdoors*, Ammi grew up in the mountains of North Idaho, where spring trilliums and fall firewood left their mark on her soul. After over a decade of global adventures that often included the luxury of electricity and running water, she returned to her hometown of Sandpoint. She lives in the forest with her husband, their two children, and a fluctuating animal-to-human ratio.

CPSIA information can be obtained
at www.ICGtesting.com
Printed in the USA
BVHW041818220223
659019BV00003B/18

9 781957 607139